THE
SQUASH &
PUMPKIN
COOKBOOK

THE
SQUASH &
PUMPKIN
COOKBOOK

HEATHER THOMAS

EBURY
PRESS

CONTENTS

SNACKS & APPETISERS

DINNERS

BAKING & DESSERTS

INTRODUCTION

When most of us think of autumn, it's not only beautiful images of the season of mists and mellow fruitfulness, with trees decked out in golden and fiery red foliage that we see. We also visualise orange pumpkins and rainbow-coloured squash stacked on roadsides and the porches of clapboard-clad houses, especially at Halloween and Thanksgiving. But although pumpkins and squash are seasonal vegetables that appear in autumn and last through winter into spring, they are now grown all over the world and so are available throughout the year.

Pumpkin and squash are members of the cucurbit family (they are distant cousins of melons and cucumbers), and are among the oldest domesticated plants. They are so versatile that nearly every part can be eaten, from the flowers to the outer skin, flesh and seeds. The main difference between pumpkins and squash, apart from their size and colour, is that the flesh of the pumpkin is more fibrous. However, they both have a sweet, nutty flavour and can be used interchangeably in most of the recipes featured in this book.

VARIETIES

The most common variety of squash on sale is the butternut squash, but you can also buy spaghetti squash (which has fibrous, noodle-like strands and can be used as a great low-carb substitute for pasta), acorn squash, turban squash, carnival squash and small round gem squashes that are perfect for stuffing and baking. The best pumpkins for cooking are not the giant ones that are usually carved into lanterns for Halloween, but the smaller, sweeter ones, which are grown for maximum flavour rather than size.

NUTRITIONAL GOODNESS

Fat-free, cholesterol-free, sodium-free, low in calories and high in fibre, pumpkin and squash can play an important role in a healthy varied diet. They are a good source of vitamins A, C and E, plus a jackpot of minerals – manganese, iron, zinc, magnesium and potassium. The edible seeds are also packed with minerals, as well as protein, fibre and healthy heart-friendly monounsaturated fatty acids.

CHOOSING PUMPKIN & SQUASH

As a rule of thumb, the larger the pumpkin, the less flavour it has, and the more fibrous and watery it's likely to be, so choose large pumpkins for decoration and smaller ones for cooking. If you're planning on eating a pumpkin, choose one with hard skin and without any soft spots or cracks. When selecting squash, always choose one with smooth, unblemished skin and no dents, cracks, cuts or soft spots. They should feel particularly heavy for their size (if they're too light, they're either not ripe yet, or already past their prime). The colour should be uniform, rich and deep. Butternut squash should not have any green on the skin, while acorn squash should be uniformly green – if there's too much orange, it's overripe. Spaghetti squash should be yellow all over, with no soft spots, cracks or blemishes.

Ready-to-eat butternut squash weigh anything between 450g/1lb and 2.25kg/5lb. A medium squash would be around the middle of this weight range. Note that after peeling and deseeding, the squash (flesh) will weigh 50–75g/2–3oz) less.

COOKING & PREPARING PUMPKIN & SQUASH

Pumpkins and squash are so versatile that you can bake, roast, fry, stir-fry, grill (broil), barbecue, purée, candy or stuff them. You can add them to soups, stews and curries, bake them in gratins, cakes and cookies, or turn them into delicious sweet pies or savoury scones. You will find recipes for all of these in the following pages, as well as for salads, risottos, gnocchi, pasta dishes and snacks. We also have special Halloween and Thanksgiving recipes, plus lots of delicious ideas for using up leftover pumpkins and the scooped-out flesh from carved jack-o'-lanterns. Nothing gets wasted!

Below are some basic instructions for different cooking methods.

BOILING
Peel the pumpkin or squash and remove the seeds, then cut the flesh into 2.5cm/1in chunks and cook in a saucepan of boiling salted water for 10–12 minutes, or until tender. Drain well.

STEAMING
Prepare the pumpkin or squash as above, then cook in a steamer basket over a saucepan of boiling water for 10–12 minutes.

MICROWAVING

Prepare the pumpkin or squash as above, then place in a microwaveable bowl with 1 tablespoon water. Cover with cling film (plastic wrap) and pierce a few times with a knife. Microwave on high for 6–7 minutes until tender, then drain.

ROASTING

Peel and deseed the pumpkin or squash, then cut into cubes, wedges or slices and arrange in a single layer on a baking tray (cookie sheet) lined with baking parchment. Drizzle with oil, season with sea salt and freshly ground black pepper and sprinkle with ground spices, seeds or herbs (if you wish). Roast in a preheated oven (usually at 200°C/400°F/gas mark 6) for approximately 30 minutes (for cubes) or up to 1 hour (for large wedges).

MASHING AND PURÉEING

Many of the recipes in this book use mashed or puréed pumpkin or squash. First, boil, steam or microwave it (see above) until tender, then drain and mash with a potato masher or push through a food mill. Alternatively, the cooked pumpkin or squash can be blitzed in a blender or food processor for a smoother purée. If you wish, you can flavour it with sea salt and freshly ground black pepper, and herbs, ground spices, butter or cream. Alternatively, you can keep a can of pumpkin purée in your store cupboard for when you're baking and don't have any fresh.

DRYING AND TOASTING PUMPKIN SEEDS

Instead of discarding them, why not dry the seeds from inside a fresh pumpkin? Either leave them out in the sunshine to dry, or place them in small bowls and leave on a warm windowsill or in an airing cupboard (closet) overnight.

To toast them, set a heavy-based frying pan (skillet) over a low to medium heat. When the pan is hot, add the seeds and agitate them gently in the pan until they release their aroma and start to change colour. Remove from the heat immediately before they catch and burn. Leave to cool, then store in a sealed container in the fridge for up to 3–4 weeks. Use them as a topping for yoghurt, porridge, soups, stir-fries and salads, or add them to homemade granola, trail mix and energy and protein bars.

LIGHT MEALS

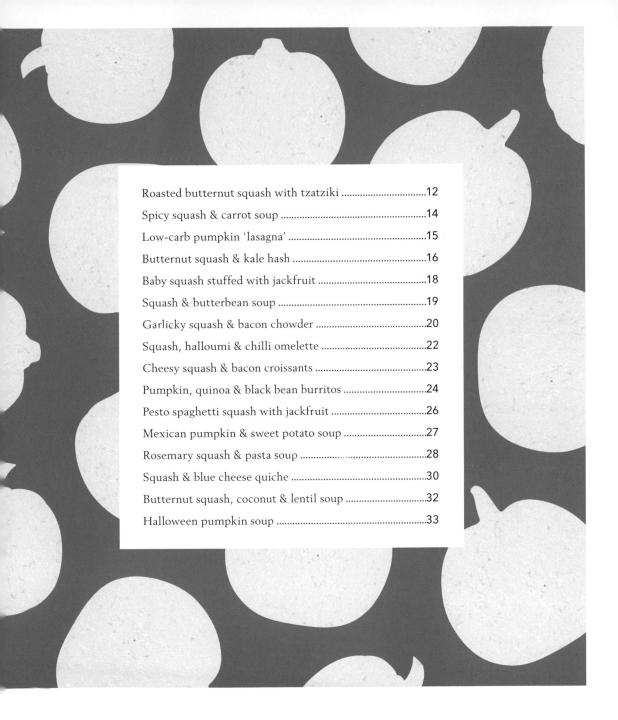

ROASTED BUTTERNUT SQUASH WITH TZATZIKI

SERVES: 4 | **PREP:** 15 MINUTES + 30 MINUTES TO DRAIN | **COOK:** 40-45 MINUTES

4 small butternut squashes
1 tbsp olive oil, plus extra
    for brushing
125g/4oz (½ cup) pancetta
    cubes
1 red onion, diced
2 garlic cloves, crushed
1 x 400g/14oz can
    chickpeas (garbanzos),
    rinsed and drained
100g/3½oz baby spinach
a squeeze of lemon juice
sea salt and freshly ground
    black pepper

For the tzatziki:
½ cucumber, coarsely grated
2 garlic cloves, crushed
1 tbsp olive oil
250g/9oz (generous 1 cup)
    Greek yoghurt
juice of ½ small lemon
a small bunch of mint,
    finely chopped

TIP: If you roast the squash halves cut-side down, they will be even more golden brown.

One of the easiest ways to cook butternut squash is to roast it, either whole, halved or cut into quarters. You can brush it with oil or melted butter, then sprinkle with dried or fresh herbs or even spices. In this recipe, we've served the squash topped with healthy garlicky chickpeas and crispy pancetta.

1 Begin by making the tzatziki. Put the grated cucumber in a sieve or colander over a bowl and sprinkle with a little salt. Stir lightly and leave for 30 minutes to draw out the moisture. Squeeze out any remaining water, then transfer the cucumber to a clean bowl and stir in the garlic, oil, yoghurt, lemon juice and mint. Season to taste.

2 Preheat the oven to 180°C/350°F/gas mark 4.

3 Cut each butternut squash in half lengthways and remove the seeds. Place on a baking tray (cookie sheet), cut-side up, and brush with olive oil. Season with salt and pepper, then roast for 40–45 minutes until golden brown and softened.

4 Meanwhile, set a large frying pan (skillet) over a medium to high heat and cook the pancetta for 4–5 minutes, tossing and turning, until it is golden brown and the fat has run out. Remove from the pan and set aside on a plate.

5 Add the olive oil, onion and garlic to the same pan and cook over a medium heat for 6–8 minutes, or until tender. Reduce the heat and stir in the chickpeas. Cook gently for 2 minutes, then add the spinach. When it turns bright green and wilts into the mixture, add the lemon juice and season to taste.

6 Serve the roasted squash topped with the chickpea mixture and crispy pancetta, with some tzatziki on the side.

SPICY SQUASH & CARROT SOUP

SERVES: 4 | **PREP:** 20 MINUTES | **COOK:** 35 MINUTES

3 tbsp olive oil
1 onion, chopped
2 garlic cloves, crushed
2.5cm/1in piece of fresh root
    ginger, peeled and diced
4 large carrots, chopped
3 celery sticks, diced
500g/1lb 2oz butternut
    squash, peeled, deseeded
    and diced
600ml/1 pint (2½ cups) hot
    vegetable stock (broth)
300ml/½ pint (1¼ cups)
    canned coconut milk
2 tsp ground turmeric
½ tsp ground cumin
freshly grated nutmeg
a handful of parsley,
    finely chopped
sea salt and freshly ground
    black pepper

For the chilli oil:
2 tbsp extra virgin olive oil
a good pinch of crushed
    dried chilli flakes

The chilli oil adds a dash of heat to this warming winter soup. It's surprisingly filling, especially if you serve it with crusty bread. Plus it's so healthy: the butternut squash, fresh ginger, turmeric and coconut milk are all good sources of antioxidants and are anti-inflammatory.

1 Begin by making the chilli oil. Put the oil and chilli flakes in a small bowl and stir well. Set aside while you make the soup. The chilli will permeate the olive oil, turning it red and spicy.

2 To make the soup, heat the oil in a large saucepan set over a low to medium heat. Add the onion, garlic, ginger, carrots and celery, and cook for 10 minutes, stirring occasionally, until tender but not coloured. Stir in the squash and cook for a further 5 minutes.

3 Add the hot stock and bring to the boil. Reduce the heat immediately and simmer for 15 minutes, or until all the vegetables are tender.

4 Blitz the soup, in batches, in a blender or food processor until smooth.

5 Return the soup to the pan and stir in the coconut milk and spices. Reheat gently, stirring occasionally, over a low heat. If the soup is too thick, just add a little more coconut milk. Season to taste and stir in the parsley.

6 Divide between 4 shallow bowls and drizzle with the chilli oil. Serve immediately.

OR YOU CAN TRY THIS...
– Use pumpkin instead of squash.
– Add some paprika, cinnamon or ground coriander.
– Use ground ginger instead of fresh.

LOW-CARB PUMPKIN 'LASAGNA'

SERVES: 4 | **PREP:** 20 MINUTES | **COOK:** 1 HOUR

3 tbsp olive oil, plus extra
  for brushing
1 large onion, finely chopped
3 garlic cloves, crushed
400g/14oz white or chestnut
  mushrooms, sliced
2 x 400g/14oz cans chopped
  tomatoes
2 tbsp tomato purée (paste)
a good pinch of dried
  oregano
400g/14oz spinach, chopped
a few drops of balsamic
  vinegar
500g/1lb 2oz pumpkin,
  peeled, deseeded and
  very thinly sliced (use a
  mandolin, if you have one)
4 tbsp grated Parmesan
  cheese
sea salt and freshly ground
  black pepper

For the white sauce:
30g/1oz (2 tbsp) butter
30g/1oz (¼ cup) plain
  (all-purpose) flour
300ml/½ pint (1¼ cups) milk
a pinch of grated nutmeg

In this cheat's lasagna, slices of pumpkin replace the traditional pasta sheets to make a lighter dish with a lower carb content. Serve with a crisp salad.

1 Preheat the oven to 200°C/400°F/gas mark 6.

2 Heat the oil in a large frying pan (skillet) set over a medium heat. Add the onion and garlic and cook, stirring occasionally, for 6–8 minutes, or until tender. Stir in the mushrooms and cook for a further 3–4 minutes until golden.

3 Add the tomatoes, tomato purée and oregano and cook for 5 minutes, or until the mixture thickens and reduces. Stir in the spinach and let it wilt into the mixture and turn bright green. Season to taste with salt and pepper and a few drops of balsamic vinegar and turn off the heat.

4 To make the white sauce, melt the butter in a saucepan set over a low heat and stir in the flour. Cook for 2 minutes, then gradually whisk in the milk with a balloon whisk to prevent any lumps. Bring to the boil, stirring all the time, then reduce the heat and simmer for 3–5 minutes until the sauce thickens. Stir in the nutmeg and season to taste.

5 Lightly brush an ovenproof baking dish with oil and cover the base with a layer of overlapping pumpkin slices, then spoon over a layer of the mushroom and tomato sauce. Continue layering up the dish in this way, finishing with a layer of pumpkin. Pour the white sauce over the top and sprinkle with Parmesan.

6 Bake for 25–30 minutes, or until the lasagna is bubbling and golden brown and the pumpkin is tender. Serve immediately.

OR YOU CAN TRY THIS...
– Use a large butternut squash instead of pumpkin.
– Instead of making this with the veggie tomato and mushroom sauce, use ragu.

BUTTERNUT SQUASH & KALE HASH

SERVES: 4 | **PREP:** 10 MINUTES | **COOK:** 25-30 MINUTES

600g/1lb 5oz butternut
squash, peeled, deseeded
and cubed
200g/7oz kale, shredded
2 tbsp olive oil
1 red onion, diced
2 garlic cloves, crushed
1 red chilli, deseeded and
shredded
1 tsp fennel seeds
4 medium free-range eggs
sea salt and freshly ground
black pepper
hot sauce, to serve
(optional)

This healthy hash is great for a midweek supper or weekend brunch. It's very versatile, and you can add leftover cooked vegetables so as not to waste them.

1 Cook the butternut squash in a large saucepan of lightly salted boiling water for about 10 minutes, or until just tender. Remove with a slotted spoon and drain well. Add the kale to the boiling water in the pan and cook for 2–3 minutes, or until tender but still crisp. Remove from the pan and rinse under cold water, then drain well.

2 Heat the oil in a large frying pan (skillet) set over a low to medium heat. Cook the onion, garlic and chilli, stirring occasionally, for 5 minutes without browning. Stir in the fennel seeds, squash and kale, spreading it out in the pan and pressing down with a spatula into a single layer. Cook for 5–10 minutes until crisp and golden brown underneath. Turn it over and cook on the other side.

3 Meanwhile, break the eggs into a saucepan of simmering water and poach for 3–4 minutes until the whites are set and the yolks are still runny. Remove with a slotted spoon and set aside on a plate lined with kitchen paper (paper towels) to drain.

4 Divide the hash between 4 serving plates and top each one with a poached egg. Season with salt and pepper and serve immediately, drizzled with hot sauce, if wished.

OR YOU CAN TRY THIS...
– Use pumpkin or sweet potato instead of squash.
– Substitute cabbage, spring greens or cavolo nero for the kale.

BABY SQUASH STUFFED WITH JACKFRUIT

SERVES: 4 | **PREP:** 20 MINUTES | **COOK:** 40-45 MINUTES

4 small butternut or acorn
squashes, halved and
deseeded
4 tbsp olive oil, plus extra
for brushing
2 tbsp maple syrup
1 onion, finely chopped
2 garlic cloves, crushed
1 tsp cumin seeds
1 tsp smoked paprika
1 tsp chilli powder
1 red (bell) pepper,
deseeded and diced
1 tbsp tomato purée (paste)
1 x 400g/14oz can green
jackfruit, drained and
sliced
2 ripe tomatoes, diced
150g/5oz baby spinach
250g/9oz (1 cup) cooked
brown rice
a few coriander (cilantro)
sprigs, chopped
75g/3oz (¾ cup) grated
cheese, e.g. Cheddar
sea salt and freshly ground
black pepper

TIP: If you're vegan, omit
the cheese or use a cashew
cheese substitute.

Jackfruit is a great 'faux meat' substitute for vegetarians, vegans and
anyone who wants to cut down on their meat consumption. You can
buy it in cans (in water or brine) in many supermarkets, delis and
health food stores.

1 Preheat the oven to 200°C/400°F/gas mark 6

2 With a sharp knife, score a diagonal pattern into the flesh of each
squash half. Lightly brush with 2 tablespoons of the olive oil and the
maple syrup. Place them on a baking tray (cookie sheet), cut-side up,
and bake for 35–40 minutes, or until tender.

3 Meanwhile, heat the remaining oil in a large frying pan (skillet) set
over a medium heat. Add the onion and garlic and cook, stirring
occasionally, for 6–8 minutes. Stir in the spices and red pepper and
cook for a further 5 minutes.

4 Add the tomato purée, jackfruit and tomatoes and cook for a
further 10 minutes. Use 2 forks to shred the jackfruit, then stir in
the spinach and cook for 2 minutes until it wilts. Add the rice and
coriander and stir to combine.

5 Scoop out the flesh in the centre of each baked squash half, leaving
a thin border around the outside. Dice the flesh and stir it into the
jackfruit and rice mixture. Season to taste with salt and pepper.

6 Divide the mixture between the hollowed-out squash halves.
Sprinkle the cheese over the top and flash under a hot grill (broiler)
until melted, bubbling and golden brown. Serve immediately.

OR YOU CAN TRY THIS...

– Add some chopped pecans or walnuts.
– Use cooked quinoa instead of rice.

SQUASH & BUTTERBEAN SOUP

SERVES: 4 | **PREP:** 20 MINUTES | **COOK:** 35-40 MINUTES

2 tbsp olive oil
1 large onion, finely chopped
2 garlic cloves, crushed
1 celery stick, diced
1 large carrot, thinly sliced
900g/2lb butternut squash, peeled, deseeded and cubed
a pinch of crushed dried chilli flakes
1 tsp smoked paprika
1 tsp ground turmeric
½ tsp grated nutmeg
1.1 litres/2 pints (5 cups) hot vegetable stock (broth)
1 x 400g/14oz can butterbeans (lima beans), rinsed and drained
sea salt and freshly ground black pepper
chopped coriander (cilantro), for sprinkling

For the spicy onion topping:
2 tbsp olive oil
1 red onion, thinly sliced
2 garlic cloves, crushed
1 red chilli, shredded
1 tsp yellow mustard seeds
1 tsp cumin seeds

This is the perfect autumnal soup – warming, spicy and a good source of vegetable protein and zinc. If you've been making jack-o'-lanterns for Halloween, why not substitute pumpkin for the squash? It's a delicious way to use up all the scooped-out flesh.

1 Heat the oil in a large saucepan set over a low heat. Add the onion, garlic and celery and cook, stirring occasionally, for 6–8 minutes until softened. Add the carrot and squash and cook, stirring occasionally, for a further 5 minutes. Stir in the chilli flakes and ground spices and cook for 1 minute.

2 Add the hot stock and bring to the boil, then simmer gently for 15 minutes, or until the vegetables are tender. Add half the beans to the soup.

3 Meanwhile, to make the spicy onion topping, heat the oil in a frying pan (skillet) set over a low heat. Add the onion and cook, stirring occasionally, for 10 minutes, or until really tender and golden brown. Add the garlic, chilli and mustard and cumin seeds and increase the heat. Cook for 1–2 minutes until the mustard seeds start popping.

4 Blitz the soup in a blender or food processor until smooth. Return to the pan and stir in the remaining beans. Season to taste with salt and pepper and set over a low heat to gently heat through.

5 Ladle the soup into bowls and add a spoonful of the spicy onion topping to each one. Sprinkle with coriander and serve immediately.

OR YOU CAN TRY THIS...
– Use any white beans, e.g. cannellini or haricot beans.
– Sprinkle with grated Cheddar cheese instead of the spicy onion topping.

TIP: This soup freezes well and will keep in the freezer for up to 3 months.

GARLICKY SQUASH & BACON CHOWDER

SERVES: 4 | **PREP:** 15 MINUTES | **COOK:** 35 MINUTES

200g/7oz bacon lardons
   or pancetta cubes
1 tbsp olive oil
1 onion, finely chopped
1 celery stick, diced
4 large garlic cloves, crushed
2 leeks, trimmed and thinly
   sliced
1 large butternut squash,
   peeled, deseeded and
   diced
1 heaped tbsp plain
   (all-purpose) flour
600ml/1 pint (2½ cups)
   milk
150ml/¼ pint (generous
   ½ cup) vegetable stock
   (broth)
1 bay leaf
a handful of flat-leaf parsley,
   finely chopped
sea salt and freshly ground
   black pepper

This creamy soup is very filling and makes a good meal-in-a-bowl on a cold day. The squash makes a tasty and colourful change from potatoes, which are normally used.

1 Heat a large saucepan over a medium heat. When it's hot, add the bacon or pancetta. Cook for 3 minutes, stirring, until the fat runs out and the bacon or pancetta is crispy and golden brown.

2 Add the oil, then stir in the onion, celery, garlic and leeks. Cook, stirring occasionally, for 5 minutes until softened. Add the squash and cook for a further 3 minutes.

3 Stir in the flour, then cook for 2 minutes without browning. Add the milk and stock, a little at a time, together with the bay leaf, and stir until well mixed and smooth. Bring to the boil, stirring constantly, then reduce the heat to low and simmer gently for 15 minutes, or until the vegetables are cooked through and tender.

4 Stir in the parsley and season to taste with salt and pepper. Ladle into shallow bowls and serve immediately.

OR YOU CAN TRY THIS...
– Use pumpkin instead of squash.
– Add some canned sweetcorn kernels.
– For a creamier texture and flavour, stir in some crème fraîche at the end.

TIP: The soup can be cooled and then transferred to a sealed container and frozen for up to 3 months.

SQUASH, HALLOUMI & CHILLI OMELETTE

SERVES: 4 | **PREP:** 15 MINUTES | **COOK:** 25-30 MINUTES

450g/1lb butternut squash, peeled, deseeded and diced

2 tbsp olive oil

6 spring onions (scallions), thinly sliced

1 red (bell) pepper, deseeded and chopped

2 garlic cloves, crushed

1 red chilli, deseeded and diced

150g/5oz spinach, shredded

150g/5oz halloumi, cubed

6 medium free-range eggs, beaten

sea salt and freshly ground black pepper

You can serve this delicious omelette hot or lukewarm for lunch, brunch or a light supper, or enjoy it cold for a packed lunch or picnic. It keeps well in an airtight container in the fridge overnight.

1 Cook the butternut squash in a saucepan of lightly salted boiling water for 6–8 minutes, or until it's just tender but still holds its shape. Drain well.

2 Heat the oil in a large non-stick frying pan (skillet) with a heatproof handle set over a low to medium heat. Add the spring onions, red pepper and garlic and cook, stirring occasionally, for 6–8 minutes until softened but not browned. Add the chilli, drained squash, spinach and halloumi, and cook for a further 3–4 minutes, stirring occasionally, until the vegetables are cooked and the halloumi is golden brown.

3 Pour the beaten eggs into the pan, swirling them around, and reduce the heat. Season with salt and pepper and cook gently for 5–6 minutes until the omelette is set and golden brown underneath.

4 While the omelette is cooking, preheat the grill (broiler) to a high heat. Pop the pan under the grill for 4–5 minutes until the top of the omelette is set, golden brown and puffed up.

5 Slide the omelette out of the pan onto a wooden board and cut into wedges. Serve hot or lukewarm with salad.

OR YOU CAN TRY THIS...

– Use pumpkin or sweet potato instead of squash.
– Add some diced chorizo or pancetta.

CHEESY SQUASH & BACON CROISSANTS

SERVES: 4 | **PREP:** 10 MINUTES | **COOK:** 15 MINUTES

300g/10oz butternut
squash, peeled, deseeded
and thinly sliced
8 thin streaky bacon rashers
(slices)
olive oil, for drizzling
leaves from a few thyme
sprigs
4 large croissants
4 tbsp low-fat soft cheese
4 tsp green pesto
sea salt and freshly ground
black pepper

These hot savoury croissants make a delicious snack or light lunch. They're quick and easy to prepare and cook, and a great way of using up some leftover squash lurking in the back of the fridge.

1 Preheat the oven to 220°C/425°F/gas mark 7. Line 2 baking trays (cookie sheets) with baking parchment.

2 Arrange the squash and bacon on one of the lined trays. Drizzle with olive oil and sprinkle the thyme over the squash. Season with salt and pepper. Roast for 15 minutes, or until the bacon is golden brown and crispy and the squash is just tender and still retains its shape.

3 Place the croissants on the other tray and pop into the oven 5 minutes before the end of the cooking time – just long enough to heat them through and crisp them up.

4 Slice each croissant through the middle horizontally and spread the bottom half with soft cheese. Cover with the roast squash and crumble the crispy bacon over the top. Drizzle with pesto and cover with the top half of each croissant. Serve immediately.

OR YOU CAN TRY THIS...
– Add some rocket (arugula), baby spinach or watercress.
– Use crumbled feta or blue cheese instead of soft cheese, or roast some sliced halloumi.

PUMPKIN, QUINOA & BLACK BEAN BURRITOS

SERVES: 4 | **PREP:** 20 MINUTES | **COOK:** 25-30 MINUTES

400g/14oz pumpkin, peeled,
   deseeded and cubed
1 tbsp olive oil, plus extra
   for drizzling
75g/3oz (scant ½ cup)
   quinoa (dry weight)
a bunch of spring onions
   (scallions), thinly sliced
3 garlic cloves, crushed
1 chilli, shredded
1 red (bell) pepper,
   deseeded and thinly
   sliced
1 x 400g/14oz can black
   beans, rinsed and drained
a few coriander (cilantro)
   sprigs, chopped
juice of 1 lime
4 large wholewheat tortilla
   wraps
50g/2oz (½ cup) grated
   Cheddar or Monterey
   Jack cheese
sea salt and freshly ground
   black pepper
sour cream and hot salsa or
   hot sauce, to serve

The quinoa, beans, wholewheat wraps and cheese provide plenty of healthy plant protein in these delicious veggie burritos. Vegans can use dairy-free yoghurt and grated vegan cheese.

1 Preheat the oven to 220°C/425°F/gas mark 7.

2 Arrange the pumpkin on a large baking tray (cookie sheet) and drizzle with oil. Season lightly with salt and pepper and roast for 25–30 minutes, or until tender but not mushy.

3 Meanwhile, cook the quinoa according to the instructions on the packet.

4 Heat the oil in a large frying pan (skillet) set over a medium heat and add the spring onions, garlic, chilli and red pepper. Cook, stirring occasionally, for 6–8 minutes. Add the beans and cook for a further 5 minutes until everything is heated through, then add the coriander, cooked quinoa and lime juice, and stir in the roasted pumpkin. Season to taste.

5 Meanwhile, warm the tortillas in a hot griddle pan or a microwave. Divide the pumpkin and quinoa mixture between them. Sprinkle with grated cheese and roll up or fold over to enclose the filling. Serve immediately with sour cream and salsa or hot sauce.

OR YOU CAN TRY THIS...
– Use red kidney beans instead of black beans.
– Add some grilled sliced mushrooms or red onions.
– Use squash or sweet potato instead of pumpkin.

PESTO SPAGHETTI SQUASH WITH JACKFRUIT

SERVES: 4 | **PREP:** 20 MINUTES | **COOK:** 30 MINUTES

1 medium-sized spaghetti
squash, split lengthways
and deseeded
3 tbsp olive oil, plus extra
for drizzling
300g/10oz baby plum
tomatoes, halved
1 red onion, thinly sliced
3 garlic cloves, crushed
1 x 400g/14oz can green
jackfruit in brine, drained
1 tbsp maple syrup
90ml/3fl oz (scant ½ cup)
vegetable stock (broth)
a pinch of crushed dried
chilli flakes or red pepper
flakes
400g/14oz kale, trimmed,
rinsed and coarsely
shredded
grated zest and juice of
1 lemon
4 tbsp fresh green pesto
grated Parmesan cheese,
for sprinkling
sea salt and freshly ground
black pepper

TIP: Vegans can make this
using vegan pesto and grated
vegan cheese.

**Spaghetti squash is a great low-carb, low-calorie and gluten-free
substitute for pasta. It is best eaten *al dente* (just tender, but not mushy).**

1 Preheat the oven to 200°C/400°F/gas mark 6. Line 2 baking trays
(cookie sheets) with baking parchment.

2 Prick the skin of the squash a few times with a fork. Drizzle the cut
sides lightly with oil and season with salt and pepper. Place, cut-side
down, on one of the lined baking trays.

3 Place the tomatoes, cut-side up, on the other lined baking tray.
Drizzle with olive oil and season with salt and pepper. Place both
trays in the oven for 30 minutes, or until the strands of squash are
just tender and the tomatoes are starting to char round the edges.
Remove from the oven and allow to cool a little before scraping out
the squash strands with a fork.

4 Meanwhile, heat 1 tablespoon of the oil in a frying pan (skillet) set
over a medium heat. Add the onion and 2 of the garlic cloves and
cook, stirring occasionally, for 6–8 minutes until tender. Squeeze as
much water as possible out of the jackfruit and pat dry with kitchen
paper (paper towels). Stir into the pan, along with the maple syrup
and stock, and simmer gently for 10 minutes, or until the liquid has
been absorbed. Use 2 forks to shred the jackfruit and season with
salt and pepper.

5 Heat the remaining oil in another frying pan (skillet) set over a
medium to high heat. Add the remaining garlic and the chilli or red
pepper flakes and cook for 1 minute, then stir in the kale and cook
for a further 3–4 minutes, or until it wilts. Gently stir in the lemon
zest and juice, along with the strands of squash and roasted tomatoes.
Add the pesto and toss everything together gently.

6 Divide between 4 serving bowls and top with the jackfruit. Sprinkle
with grated Parmesan and serve immediately.

MEXICAN PUMPKIN & SWEET POTATO SOUP

SERVES: 4-6 | **PREP:** 20 MINUTES | **COOK:** 40 MINUTES

3 tbsp olive oil
1 large onion, chopped
2 celery sticks, diced
3 garlic cloves, crushed
1 jalapeño chilli, deseeded
  and chopped
2 large sweet potatoes,
  peeled and cubed
500g/1lb 2oz pumpkin,
  peeled, deseeded and
  cubed
1 tsp chipotle paste or
  1 tbsp smoky chipotle
  seasoning
1 tsp ground cumin
1.1 litres/2 pints (5 cups)
  hot vegetable stock
  (broth)
½ tsp dried oregano
juice of 1 lime
4 tsp pumpkin seeds
4 tbsp crème fraîche
smoked paprika, for dusting
a few coriander (cilantro)
  sprigs, chopped
sea salt and freshly ground
  black pepper

TIP: This soup will freeze well in an airtight container for up to 3 months.

This gently spiced and smoky soup is a great way to warm up on a cold day, plus it's easy to make and keeps well in the fridge or freezer. Fresh jalapeño chillies are available in some large supermarkets and online. Chipotles are jalapeño chillies that have been smoked and dried. You can buy them whole, ground or made into paste or sauce.

1 Heat the olive oil in a large saucepan set over a medium heat. Add the onion, celery, garlic and chilli and cook, stirring occasionally, for 5 minutes until softened. Add the sweet potatoes and pumpkin and cook for a further 5 minutes. Stir in the chipotle paste or seasoning and the cumin and cook for 1 minute more.

2 Pour in the stock and bring to the boil. Reduce the heat to low, then add the oregano. Simmer gently for 20 minutes, or until the vegetables are really tender.

3 Blitz the soup in a blender or food processor until smooth, then return it to the pan and stir in the lime juice. Season to taste with salt and pepper, and heat through gently over a low heat.

4 Meanwhile, place a frying pan (skillet) over a medium to high heat. Once it's hot, add the pumpkin seeds, spreading them out in a single layer. Toast for 1–2 minutes, tossing them now and then, until golden brown and fragrant. Remove from the pan before they catch and burn.

5 Serve the soup in shallow bowls and swirl in the crème fraîche. Dust lightly with smoked paprika and sprinkle with the toasted pumpkin seeds and chopped coriander.

OR YOU CAN TRY THIS...

– Use butternut squash instead of pumpkin.
– Stir in some grated Cheddar or Monterey Jack cheese before serving.
– Serve topped with tortilla chips and a spoonful of hot salsa.

ROSEMARY SQUASH & PASTA SOUP

SERVES: 4 | **PREP:** 15 MINUTES | **COOK:** 40 MINUTES

2 tbsp olive oil
1 red onion, chopped
2 garlic cloves, crushed
500g/1lb 2oz butternut
    squash, peeled, deseeded
    and cubed
½ tsp smoked paprika
leaves from 1 rosemary
    sprig, chopped
1 litre/1¾ pints (4 cups) hot
    vegetable stock (broth)
100g/3½oz fusilli, ditalini
    or soup pasta (dry
    weight)
3–4 tbsp crème fraîche
    (optional)
4 tbsp shaved Parmesan
    cheese
sea salt and freshly ground
    black pepper

This is comfort food at its very best – a smooth and velvety soup with chunks of squash and pasta *al dente* with a spike of aromatic rosemary. If you like a creamy texture, stir in some crème fraîche just before serving.

1 Heat the olive oil in a large saucepan set over a low heat. Add the onion and garlic and cook gently, stirring occasionally, for 8–10 minutes until softened.

2 Add the butternut squash, paprika and rosemary and cook for 2–3 minutes, stirring, until the squash is glistening with oil and starting to soften a little. Pour in the stock and increase the heat to bring to the boil.

3 Reduce the heat to a gentle simmer and cook for about 15 minutes, or until the squash is cooked but not mushy – it should keep its shape. Remove 4 spoonfuls of the squash with a slotted spoon and set aside for the garnish.

4 Blitz the soup in a blender or food processor until smooth (or use a stick blender). Return it to the pan and set over a medium heat. Add the pasta and cook for 10 minutes, or until just tender. Season to taste with salt and pepper and, if wished, stir in the crème fraîche.

5 Ladle the soup into 4 serving bowls and add the reserved squash cubes. Scatter with Parmesan and serve immediately.

OR YOU CAN TRY THIS...
– Use pumpkin instead of squash.
– Add some drained canned beans for a heartier soup.

SQUASH & BLUE CHEESE QUICHE

SERVES: 6 | **PREP:** 20 MINUTES | **CHILL:** 30 MINUTES | **COOK:** 1 HOUR

600g/1lb 5oz butternut squash, peeled, deseeded and sliced
2 tbsp olive oil, plus extra for drizzling
2 onions, thinly sliced
2 garlic cloves, crushed
4 medium free-range eggs
300ml/½ pint (1¼ cups) double (heavy) cream
a good pinch of grated nutmeg
300g/10oz frozen chopped spinach, defrosted and drained well
100g/3½oz blue cheese, e.g. Roquefort or Gorgonzola, crumbled
sea salt and freshly ground black pepper

For the shortcrust pastry:
250g/9oz (scant 2½ cups) plain (all-purpose) flour, plus extra for dusting
a pinch of sea salt
125g/4oz (½ cup) butter, chilled and diced, plus extra for greasing
3–4 tbsp cold water

This looks a bit of a faff to make, but you can use ready-made shortcrust pastry (pie crust) if you're in a hurry.

1 To make the pastry, sift the flour and salt into a mixing bowl. Add the butter and use your fingers to rub it into the flour until the mixture resembles breadcrumbs. Stir in the water, a little at a time, until everything binds together and you have a smooth ball of dough. Wrap it in cling film (plastic wrap) and chill in the fridge for at least 30 minutes.

2 Meanwhile, preheat the oven to 190°C/375°F/gas mark 5. Lightly butter a deep 23cm/9in fluted tart tin.

3 Arrange the squash slices on a baking tray (cookie sheet). Drizzle with oil and season with salt and pepper. Roast for 25–30 minutes, or until tender but not mushy.

4 While the squash is roasting, heat the oil in a frying pan (skillet) set over a low heat. Add the onions and garlic and cook, stirring occasionally, for 15–20 minutes until soft, golden and starting to caramelise.

5 Meanwhile, beat the eggs in a bowl with the cream. Stir in the nutmeg and season with salt and pepper.

6 Roll out the pastry on a lightly floured surface and use it to line the tart tin. Prick the base lightly with a fork, then cover with a layer of onions and garlic. Arrange the roasted squash slices on top. Pat the spinach dry with kitchen paper (paper towels) and add to the quiche. Crumble over the blue cheese and pour the beaten egg mixture over the top.

7 Bake for 25–30 minutes until the filling is set and golden brown. Let the quiche cool a little before cutting into slices to serve.

OR YOU CAN TRY THIS...
– Use pumpkin instead of squash.
– Substitute feta or goat's cheese for the blue cheese.

BUTTERNUT SQUASH, COCONUT & LENTIL SOUP

SERVES: 4 | **PREP:** 15 MINUTES | **COOK:** 30-35 MINUTES

2 tbsp olive oil
1 large onion, chopped
2 garlic cloves, crushed
2.5cm/1in piece of fresh
    root ginger, peeled and
    grated
a pinch of crushed dried
    chilli flakes
1 tsp ground turmeric
200g/7oz (1 cup) red lentils
    (dry weight)
750ml/1¼ pints (3 cups)
    hot vegetable stock
    (broth)
400ml/14fl oz (scant 1¾ cups)
    canned reduced-fat
    coconut milk
500g/1lb 2oz butternut
    squash, peeled, deseeded
    and cubed
200g/7oz spinach or baby
    spinach, shredded
sea salt and freshly ground
    black pepper
Thai sweet chilli sauce,
    for drizzling

The lentils thicken this soup, giving it a lovely earthy flavour. They are high in plant protein and dietary fibre, as well as folic acid, potassium and magnesium. This means they support a healthy heart and gut, and can help to lower blood pressure.

1 Heat the oil in a large saucepan set over a low to medium heat. Add the onion, garlic and ginger and cook, stirring occasionally, for 6–8 minutes until softened. Stir in the chilli flakes and turmeric and cook for 1 minute more.

2 Add the lentils and stir well until glistening with oil. Add the hot stock, coconut milk and squash and increase the heat to bring to the boil. Reduce the heat to low and simmer for 15–20 minutes until the squash is tender and the lentils are softened and cooked through.

3 Transfer half of the soup to a blender or food processor and blitz until smooth. Return it to the pan with the rest of the soup and stir in the spinach. Heat through gently and season to taste with salt and pepper.

4 Ladle the soup into bowls and serve immediately, drizzled with chilli sauce.

OR YOU CAN TRY THIS...
– Add some creamy peanut butter with the coconut milk.
– Sprinkle with roasted peanuts.
– Use pumpkin instead of squash.

HALLOWEEN PUMPKIN SOUP

SERVES: 6 | **PREP:** 20 MINUTES | **COOK:** 45 MINUTES

3 tbsp olive oil

2 large red onions, thinly
sliced

2 tsp light brown sugar

3 garlic cloves, crushed

1 red chilli, deseeded and
diced

½ tsp sweet or smoked
paprika

½ tsp ground ginger

¼ tsp grated nutmeg

1kg/2¼lb pumpkin, peeled,
deseeded and cubed

600ml/1 pint (2½ cups) hot
vegetable stock (broth)

200ml/7fl oz (generous ¾
cup) low-fat crème fraîche

sea salt and freshly ground
black pepper

1 x 2kg/4½lb pumpkin,
hollowed out, to serve
(optional)

*To serve (choose from the
following):*
fried bread croutons
crushed tortilla chips
grated Cheddar or Gruyère
cheese
chopped parsley or
coriander (cilantro)
crushed dried chilli flakes

If you want to create a sensation when you serve this velvety soup, you'll need a hollowed-out pumpkin. You can make the soup in advance and then reheat it just before filling the pumpkin shell. It's the perfect centrepiece for Halloween or Bonfire Night parties.

1 Heat the oil in a large saucepan set over a low heat. Add the onions and stir in the sugar. Cook gently, stirring occasionally, for 12–15 minutes, or until the onions are golden brown and starting to caramelise.

2 Stir in the garlic and chilli and cook for 2 minutes, then stir in the spices and add the pumpkin, turning it to coat in the oil. Pour in the hot stock and bring to boil. Reduce the heat and simmer for 20 minutes, or until the pumpkin is cooked through.

3 Blitz the soup in a blender or food processor until smooth. Alternatively, leave in the pan, remove from the heat and use a hand-held stick blender.

4 Reheat the soup over a low heat and stir in the crème fraîche. Season to taste with salt and pepper.

5 If using, pour the hot soup into the hollowed-out pumpkin shell and add your chosen garnishes. Otherwise, serve in bowls topped with your garnishes of choice.

OR YOU CAN TRY THIS...
– Roast the pumpkin before adding it to the soup for a deeper flavour.
– Vary the spices: try ground cumin, coriander or turmeric.

TIP: If you can't get reduced-fat crème fraîche, just use regular.

SALADS
& SIDES

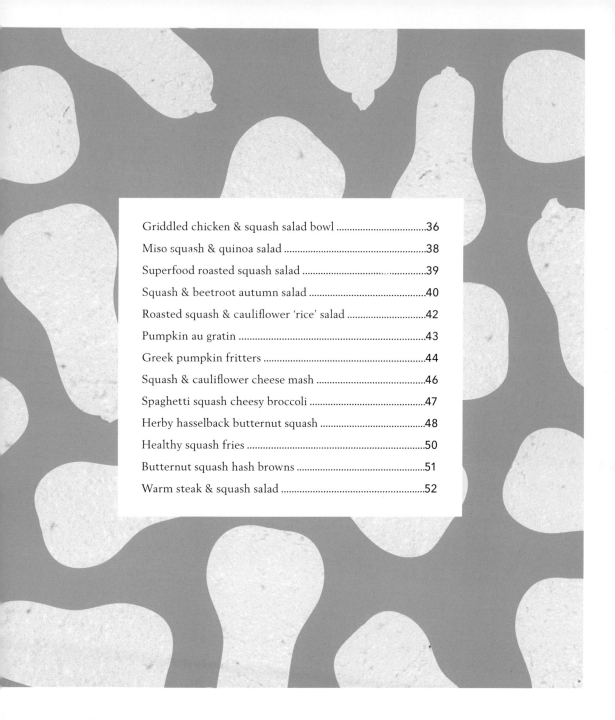

GRIDDLED CHICKEN & SQUASH SALAD BOWL

SERVES: 4 | **PREP:** 20 MINUTES | **COOK:** 25 MINUTES

1 tsp coriander seeds
2 tsp cumin seeds
500g/1lb 2oz butternut
   squash, peeled, deseeded
   and cut into thick
   matchsticks
1 red onion, cut into small
   wedges
olive oil for drizzling and
   brushing
4 skinless, boneless chicken
   breasts
250g/9oz cherry tomatoes,
   halved
½ cucumber, thickly sliced
1 ripe avocado, peeled,
   stoned (pitted) and cubed
a handful of rocket (arugula)
250g/9oz (1½ cups) cooked
   couscous
sea salt and freshly ground
   black pepper
balsamic vinegar, for drizzling
flat-leaf parsley, for sprinkling

For the seedy dressing:
3 tbsp fruity olive oil
1 tbsp white wine vinegar
juice of 1 lemon
1 garlic clove, crushed
1 tsp grated fresh root ginger
1 tsp honey mustard
1 tsp poppy seeds

This is a great meal in a bowl and it's so colourful, nutritious and healthy. If you make it in the summer, cook the vegetables and chicken on the barbecue for a smoky flavour.

1 Preheat the oven to 200°C/400°F/gas mark 6.

2 To make the seedy dressing, blitz together all the ingredients in a blender until well combined and smooth, then set aside.

3 Coarsely grind the coriander and cumin seeds in a pestle and mortar. Place the squash and red onion on a baking tray (cookie sheet) and sprinkle with the crushed seeds. Drizzle with oil and season with salt and pepper. Roast for 25 minutes, turning once or twice, until the squash and onions are tender and golden brown.

4 Meanwhile, brush a griddle pan with oil and set over a medium heat. When it's hot, add the chicken and cook for 6–8 minutes on each side, or until golden brown and cooked right through. Remove from the pan and leave to rest for a few minutes before cutting into slices.

5 Put the roasted vegetables in a large salad bowl, along with the cherry tomatoes, cucumber, avocado and rocket. Pour over the dressing and toss lightly to combine. Serve warm with the couscous and sliced chicken, drizzled with balsamic vinegar and sprinkled with parsley.

OR YOU CAN TRY THIS...
– Use pumpkin or sweet potato instead of squash.
– Substitute bulgur wheat, quinoa or brown rice for the couscous.

MISO SQUASH & QUINOA SALAD

SERVES: 4 | **PREP:** 25 MINUTES | **COOK:** 25–30 MINUTES

3 tbsp white miso paste
2 tbsp olive oil
1 tsp sesame oil
2 tsp runny honey
800g/1lb 12oz butternut
    squash, peeled, deseeded
    and cubed
150g/5oz (scant 1 cup)
    quinoa (dry weight)
a bunch of spring onions
    (scallions), thinly sliced
400g/14oz shredded greens,
    e.g. red or green cabbage,
    kale, chard or spinach
a handful of coriander
    (cilantro), chopped
seeds of ½ pomegranate
sea salt and freshly ground
    black pepper

For the dressing:
3 tbsp olive oil
2 tbsp soy sauce
juice of 2 limes
1 tbsp caster (superfine)
    sugar
a pinch of crushed dried
    chilli flakes

TIP: Vegans can use maple
syrup instead of honey.

This warm umami-flavoured salad is really nutritious, offering a jackpot of protein, healthy carbs, vitamins and minerals. It's the perfect autumnal or winter salad. If you don't have squash, use pumpkin, or even some sweet potatoes instead.

1 Preheat the oven to 220°C/425°F/gas mark 7. Line a baking tray (cookie sheet) with baking parchment.

2 In a large bowl, mix together the miso paste, olive oil, sesame oil and honey. Add the squash and stir gently until all the cubes are coated. Place them in a single layer on the lined baking tray and roast for 25–30 minutes, turning halfway through. They should be golden brown and slightly crisp on the outside and tender on the inside.

3 Meanwhile, cook the quinoa according to the instructions on the packet.

4 To make the dressing, blend all the ingredients together until well mixed.

5 Put the cooked quinoa in a large bowl with the spring onions, greens and coriander. Pour over the dressing and stir to combine, then season to taste.

6 Divide between 4 plates or serving bowls and sprinkle with pomegranate seeds. Top with the roasted squash and eat while still warm.

OR YOU CAN TRY THIS...
– Add some grated fresh root ginger to the dressing.
– Add grated carrot, toasted pine nuts and sesame seeds to the quinoa salad.
– Drizzle with soy sauce, sweet chilli sauce, tahini or pomegranate molasses.

SUPERFOOD ROASTED SQUASH SALAD

SERVES: 4 | **PREP:** 15 MINUTES | **COOK:** 25-30 MINUTES

1 large butternut squash,
    peeled, deseeded and
    cubed
olive oil, for drizzling
225g/8oz kale, trimmed
    and chopped
2 tbsp pumpkin seeds
85g/3oz (generous ½ cup)
    cashew nuts
4 spring onions (scallions),
    sliced
1 x 400g (14oz) can
    butterbeans (lima beans),
    rinsed and drained
1 ripe avocado, peeled,
    stoned (pitted) and cubed
a small bunch of flat-leaf
    parsley, chopped
sea salt and freshly ground
    black pepper

For the dressing:
4 tbsp olive oil
2 tbsp cider vinegar
1 tbsp grated fresh root
    ginger
1 garlic clove, crushed
grated zest and juice of
    1 orange
1 tsp runny honey
1 tbsp sesame seeds

This colourful salad is really healthy and nutritious. The butterbeans, seeds and cashew nuts provide plant protein, and it's packed with vitamins and essential minerals.

1 Preheat the oven to 200°C/400°F/gas mark 6.

2 Place the squash in a large roasting tray (pan). Drizzle with olive oil and season with salt and pepper. Roast for 25–30 minutes, turning once or twice, until tender and golden brown. Set aside to cool a little.

3 Meanwhile, drop the kale into a saucepan of salted boiling water. Cook for 30 seconds, then drain well.

4 Toast the pumpkin seeds and cashew nuts in a dry frying pan (skillet) set over a medium heat for 1–2 minutes, tossing gently, until golden brown. Remove immediately and set aside to cool.

5 Put the warm squash and kale in a large bowl, along with the spring onions, butterbeans and avocado. Stir in the parsley and the toasted pumpkin seeds and cashew nuts.

6 To make the dressing, mix all the ingredients together in a jug or small bowl until well blended. Season with salt and pepper. Pour over the salad and toss gently. Serve immediately while the salad is still warm.

OR YOU CAN TRY THIS...

– Use walnuts, hazelnuts or pistachios instead of cashew nuts.
– Add some pomegranate seeds.
– Sprinkle with crumbled feta, blue cheese or goat's cheese.

SQUASH & BEETROOT AUTUMN SALAD

SERVES: 4 | **PREP:** 20 MINUTES | **COOK:** 25-30 MINUTES

450g/1lb butternut squash, halved, deseeded and sliced

1 large red onion, cut into thin wedges

2 raw beetroots (beets), trimmed, peeled and cut into rounds

olive oil, for drizzling

1 radicchio, trimmed and leaves separated

a handful of wild rocket (arugula)

60g/2oz (scant ½ cup) chopped walnuts

a small bunch of dill, chopped

115g/4oz feta cheese, crumbled

sea salt and freshly ground black pepper

For the dressing:
3 tbsp fruity green olive oil
1 tbsp red wine vinegar
juice of 1 small lemon
a pinch of sugar
1 tsp honey mustard

This naturally sweet and colourful salad is perfect for a light meal, a packed lunch or even for supper if served on top of some quinoa or couscous. Leave out the feta or replace it with vegan cheese for a delicious plant-based vegan meal.

1 Preheat the oven to 200°C/400°F/gas mark 6. Line 2 baking trays (cookie sheets) with baking parchment.

2 Arrange the squash and red onion on one baking tray, and the beetroot on the other. Drizzle with olive oil and season with salt and pepper. Roast for 25–30 minutes, turning once or twice, or until tender.

3 Meanwhile, make the dressing. Mix all the ingredients together until well blended.

4 Put the cooked squash and beetroot in a large bowl, and add the radicchio, rocket and walnuts. Pour over the dressing and gently toss together. Sprinkle with the dill and check the seasoning.

5 Divide between 4 serving plates and top with the feta and roasted red onions. Serve immediately, while the salad is still warm.

OR YOU CAN TRY THIS...
– Use pumpkin instead of squash.
– Add some pomegranate seeds or sliced apples or pears.
– Drizzle with green pesto or balsamic vinegar.

ROASTED SQUASH & CAULIFLOWER 'RICE' SALAD

SERVES: 4 | **PREP:** 20 MINUTES | **COOK:** 35 MINUTES

450g/1lb butternut squash, peeled, deseeded and cubed
2 red onions, cut into wedges
4 tbsp olive oil
1 large cauliflower, trimmed and leaves removed, broken into florets
2 tbsp pumpkin seeds
2 tbsp pine nuts
2 garlic cloves, crushed
1 tbsp black mustard seeds
a pinch of crushed dried chilli flakes
100g/3½oz baby spinach
50g/2oz sun-blush tomatoes, chopped
a handful of coriander (cilantro), chopped
juice of 1 lime
sea salt and freshly ground black pepper

TIP: This keeps well in a sealed container in the fridge, and can be eaten cold for a packed lunch the following day.

Cauliflower 'rice' is easy to make and tastes delicious. It's great eaten hot or cold as part of a salad, and you can add almost anything to it for a healthy meal.

1 Preheat the oven to 200°C/400°F/gas mark 6.

2 Arrange the squash and red onions on a baking tray (cookie sheet). Drizzle with most of the olive oil and season with salt and pepper. Roast for 25–30 minutes, turning once or twice, or until tender.

3 Meanwhile, place the cauliflower florets in a food processor and pulse to create rice-sized 'grains'.

4 Set a dry frying pan (skillet) over a medium heat and toast the pumpkin seeds and pine nuts for 1–2 minutes, tossing them gently, until golden brown. Remove immediately before they catch and burn. Set the seeds aside on a plate and return the pan to the heat.

5 Add the remaining olive oil to the pan, along with the garlic and mustard seeds. Cook, stirring occasionally, for 2 minutes. Add the chilli flakes and cauliflower 'rice' and cook for a further 4–5 minutes, stirring often, until the cauliflower is warm and tender, but still slightly crunchy (al dente).

6 Transfer to a large serving bowl and stir in the spinach, sun-blush tomatoes and toasted pumpkin seeds and pine nuts. Add the roasted squash and onions, along with the coriander. Toss gently together and sprinkle with the lime juice, then season to taste with salt and pepper. Serve the salad warm.

OR YOU CAN TRY THIS...
– If you don't have sun-blush tomatoes, use fresh cherry tomatoes.
– Use roasted pumpkin or sweet potato.

PUMPKIN AU GRATIN

SERVES: 4 | **PREP:** 10 MINUTES | **COOK:** 45 MINUTES

600g/1lb 5oz pumpkin,
    peeled, deseeded and
    cut into chunks
leaves from a few
    rosemary sprigs
150ml/¼ pint (generous
    ½ cup) vegetable stock
    (broth)
6 tbsp half-fat crème fraîche
100g/3½oz (½ cup)
    mascarpone
3 tbsp pumpkin seeds
60g/2oz (1 cup) fresh white
    breadcrumbs
olive oil, for drizzling
sea salt and freshly ground
    black pepper

For the tomato sauce:
2 tbsp olive oil
1 large onion, finely
    chopped
2 garlic cloves, crushed
1 x 400g/14oz can chopped
    tomatoes
1 tbsp tomato purée (paste)
a few drops of balsamic
    vinegar

Serve this gratin as a vegetable side dish, or as a tasty meal in its own right with some salad and pasta or grains. It's delicious eaten hot or lukewarm.

1 Preheat the oven to 180°C/350°F/gas mark 4.

2 Put the pumpkin in a large ovenproof dish and sprinkle with the rosemary. Season with salt and pepper and pour the stock over the top. Bake for 30 minutes, or until just tender.

3 Meanwhile, to make the tomato sauce, heat the oil in a large frying pan (skillet) set over a low heat. Add the onion and garlic and cook, stirring occasionally, for 8–10 minutes, or until softened. Add the tomatoes and tomato purée (paste) and simmer for 10 minutes, or until the sauce reduces and thickens. Add the balsamic vinegar and season with salt and pepper to taste.

4 Pour the tomato sauce over the baked pumpkin and top with dollops of crème fraîche and mascarpone. Sprinkle with the pumpkin seeds and breadcrumbs, and drizzle with olive oil.

5 Bake for 20 minutes, or until it is crisp and golden brown on top and the sauce is bubbling up. Serve immediately with a crisp salad.

OR YOU CAN TRY THIS...
– Use swede, butternut squash, parsnips or sweet potato instead of pumpkin.
– Instead of mascarpone, use crumbled feta, blue cheese or goat's cheese.

TIP: You can prepare the gratin up to and including step 4 and then leave it for 1–2 hours before baking.

GREEK PUMPKIN FRITTERS

SERVES: 4 | **PREP:** 15 MINUTES | **COOK:** 15 MINUTES

light olive oil, for shallow-frying
450g/1lb pumpkin, peeled, deseeded and cut into 5mm/¼in slices
100g/3½oz soft goat's cheese
runny Greek thyme honey, for drizzling
sea salt

For the batter:
115g/4oz (1 cup) plain (all-purpose) flour
1 tsp baking powder
a pinch of sea salt
1 medium free-range egg, beaten
1 tbsp olive oil
150ml/¼ pint (generous ½ cup) water

These pumpkin fritters are cooked in a really light batter until they are appetisingly crisp and golden. You can enjoy them as a side dish or snack, or as a first course, served with tzatziki and dressed salad leaves.

1 Begin by making the batter. Sift the flour, baking powder and salt into a bowl. Beat the egg and olive oil into the flour with a little of the water, then gradually beat in the rest of the water, a little at a time, until the batter is smooth and free from lumps.

2 Set a large, heavy frying pan (skillet) over a medium heat and pour in enough oil to reach a depth of 3mm/⅛in.

3 Dip a few of the pumpkin slices into the batter to coat them lightly all over, then fry in the pan in a single layer for 2–3 minutes until crisp and golden brown underneath. Turn them over and cook on the other side. Remove with a slotted spoon and set aside on a plate lined with kitchen paper (paper towels) to drain. Keep warm while you batter and cook the remaining pumpkin slices in the same way, working in batches.

4 Sprinkle the fritters lightly with sea salt, then crumble some goat's cheese over the top, drizzle with honey and serve immediately.

OR YOU CAN TRY THIS...
– Serve with Greek yoghurt or labneh.
– Add a pinch of dried oregano to the batter.
– Use butternut squash instead of pumpkin.

HERBY HASSELBACK BUTTERNUT SQUASH

SERVES: 4 | **PREP:** 15 MINUTES | **COOK:** 1 HOUR

1 medium butternut squash, peeled, halved and deseeded
3 tbsp unsalted butter
2 tbsp maple syrup or runny honey
2 tsp chopped lemon thyme leaves, plus extra for sprinkling
crushed dried chilli flakes, for sprinkling
sea salt and freshly ground black pepper

Prepared and cooked in this way, a butternut squash makes an attractive and delicious side dish for a roast and will be much admired by your guests. It's a little bit time-consuming to make, but well worth the effort.

1 Preheat the oven to 220°C/425°F/gas mark 7. Line a baking tray (cookie sheet) with baking parchment.

2 Place one half of the squash, flat-side down, on a chopping board and place a spoon or a chopstick on each long side of the squash. This will stop you cutting right through it.

3 Starting at one end of the squash half, use a sharp knife to make deep cuts across it horizontally, while taking care not to cut right through it. The cuts should be approximately 3–6mm/⅛–¼in apart. Keep cutting until you reach the other end of the squash, then repeat with the other squash half. Place both squash halves, flat-side up, on the lined baking tray.

4 Heat the butter, maple syrup or honey and thyme in a small saucepan set over a low heat, stirring until the butter melts and blends with the honey or syrup. Brush some of this glaze over the squash halves.

5 Roast for about 1 hour, basting 3–4 times, or until the squash is cooked, tender and golden brown.

6 Serve immediately, sprinkled with chilli flakes and thyme leaves.

TIP: You can remove the skin from the squash with a potato peeler.

OR YOU CAN TRY THIS...
– Use finely chopped sage or oregano instead of thyme.
– Add a dash of balsamic vinegar to the buttery glaze.
– Sprinkle with crumbled feta cheese.

HEALTHY SQUASH FRIES

SERVES: 4-6 | **PREP:** 10 MINUTES | **COOK:** 25-35 MINUTES

1 large butternut squash
   (approx. 900g/2lb),
   peeled, halved
   lengthways and deseeded
olive oil spray
sea salt
tomato ketchup or
   mayonnaise, to serve

These crisp golden brown 'fries' are irresistible – and you can feel free to indulge yourself and eat as many as you like. Why? Because they are baked in the oven with minimal oil instead of being deep-fried. They are so easy to make, and you can flavour them in many different ways (see suggestions below).

1 Preheat the oven to 220°C/425°F/gas mark 7. Line a baking tray (cookie sheet) with baking parchment.

2 Cut the squash halves into chips (like French fries), keeping them all a similar thickness and length, so they cook evenly.

3 Arrange them in a single layer on the lined baking tray and spray lightly with olive oil. Sprinkle with a little salt.

4 Bake for 25–35 minutes, turning halfway through, until the fries are crisp and golden brown on the outside and tender on the inside.

5 Serve immediately with ketchup, mayonnaise or your favourite sauce or dip.

OR YOU CAN TRY THIS...

– Before baking, sprinkle the squash with ready-made Cajun seasoning, or dust with smoked paprika and finely chopped rosemary, thyme or oregano.
– Serve with a pesto or honey mustard dip.

BUTTERNUT SQUASH HASH BROWNS

SERVES: 4 | **PREP:** 5 MINUTES | **COOK:** 15 MINUTES

450g/1lb butternut squash, peeled, deseeded and coarsely grated

1 garlic clove, crushed (optional)

2 medium free-range eggs, beaten

a good pinch of dried thyme

2 tbsp plain (all-purpose) flour

2 tbsp light olive oil

sea salt and freshly ground black pepper

To serve:
fried or poached eggs
crispy bacon rashers (slices)
sliced or cubed avocado

These crisp hash browns don't take long to prepare and cook, and they make a fantastic weekend breakfast or brunch.

1 In a bowl, mix together the grated squash, garlic (if using), beaten eggs and thyme. Stir in the flour until the mixture is smooth and free from lumps. Season lightly with salt and pepper.

2 Heat the oil in a large non-stick frying pan (skillet) set over a medium heat. When the pan is really hot, add a tablespoon-sized dollop of the squash batter to the pan. Allowing them some space to spread out, add another one or two dollops, depending on the size of your pan. Flatten each one with a spatula and cook for 2–3 minutes until set and golden brown underneath. Flip them over and cook on the other side.

3 Remove the hash browns from the pan and set aside to drain on a plate lined with kitchen paper (paper towels). Keep warm while you cook the remaining squash batter.

4 Serve the hash browns immediately with fried or poached eggs, bacon and avocado.

OR YOU CAN TRY THIS...
– Use grated pumpkin instead of squash.
– Serve with Greek yoghurt or drizzle with hot sauce.

WARM STEAK & SQUASH SALAD

SERVES: 4 | **PREP:** 15 MINUTES | **COOK:** 40 MINUTES

2 tbsp coriander seeds
2 tbsp cumin seeds
1 large butternut squash, deseeded and cut into strips
4 tbsp olive oil, plus extra for drizzling
450g/1lb lean steak, e.g. fillet or sirloin, all fat removed
a large handful of wild rocket (arugula)
seeds of 1 pomegranate
sea salt and freshly ground black pepper

For the dressing:
2 tbsp red wine vinegar
3 tbsp pomegranate molasses
1 tbsp Dijon mustard
2 tsp runny honey
100ml/3½fl oz (scant ½ cup) olive oil

This is a lovely autumn salad for when the days are shorter and you want something more substantial than salad leaves and tomatoes. Make it with seasonal squash – or pumpkin – and ruby-red pomegranate seeds.

1 Preheat the oven to 200°C/400°F/gas mark 6.

2 Coarsely grind the coriander and cumin seeds in a pestle and mortar. Place the squash in a large roasting tray (pan) and sprinkle the crushed seeds over the top. Drizzle with olive oil and season with salt and pepper. Roast for 25–30 minutes, turning once or twice, until tender and golden brown. Set aside to cool a little.

3 Meanwhile, make the dressing. In a bowl or jug, whisk together the vinegar, pomegranate molasses, mustard and honey. Gradually whisk in the oil and season with salt and pepper. Set aside.

4 Brush the steak with the olive oil, rubbing it into both sides, and season with salt and pepper.

5 Set a griddle pan over a high heat and, once it's really hot, add the steak. Sear for 2–3 minutes on each side for rare meat, or 4–5 minutes for medium-rare to medium. Remove from the pan and let the steak rest for 5 minutes before slicing thinly.

6 In a large bowl, lightly toss the squash, rocket and most of the pomegranate seeds with half of the dressing. Divide between 4 serving plates and top with the steak slices. Drizzle the remaining dressing over the top and sprinkle with the rest of the pomegranate seeds. Serve lukewarm.

OR YOU CAN TRY THIS...
– Use pumpkin or sweet potato.
– Drizzle with good balsamic vinegar before serving.

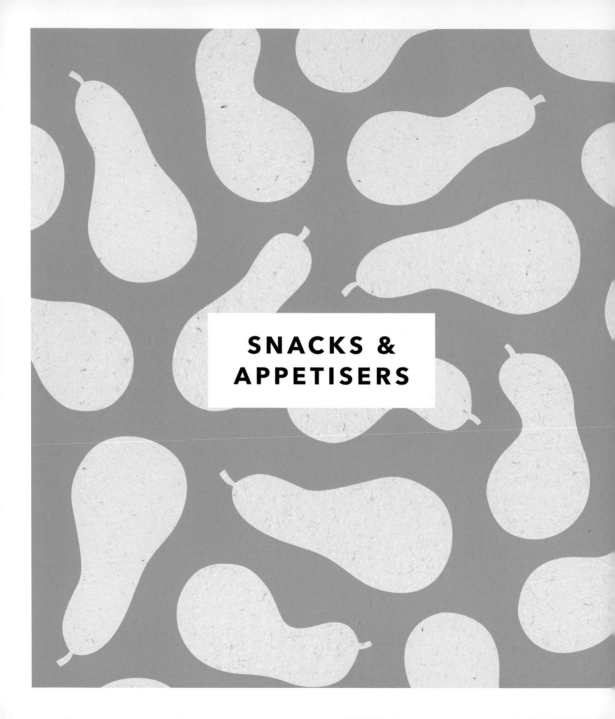

SNACKS & APPETISERS

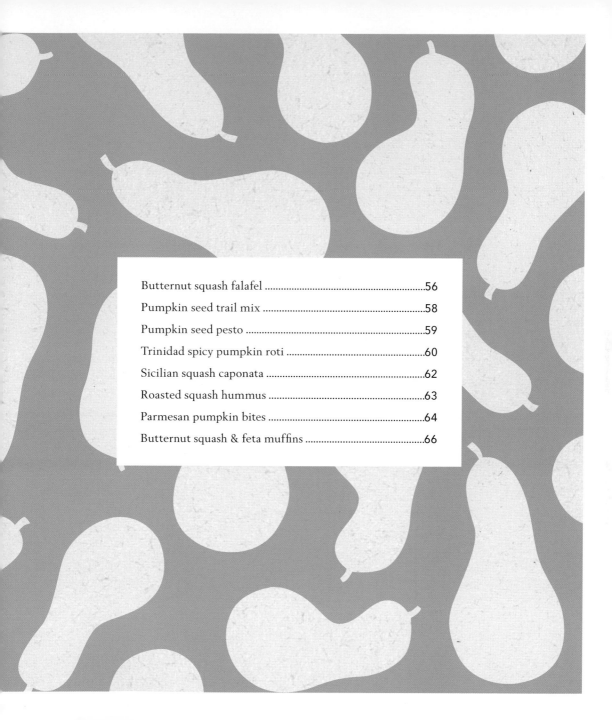

BUTTERNUT SQUASH FALAFEL

MAKES: APPROX. 24 | **SOAK:** OVERNIGHT | **PREP:** 20 MINUTES | **CHILL:** 30 MINUTES
COOK: 12-15 MINUTES

300g/10oz (generous 1¼ cups) dried chickpeas (garbanzos) (dry weight)
225g/8oz butternut squash, peeled, deseeded and cubed
½ red onion, chopped
a good handful of coriander (cilantro), chopped
2 garlic cloves, crushed
3 tbsp chickpea (gram) flour
1 tsp baking powder
1 tsp ground cumin
1 tsp ground coriander
½ tsp ground cinnamon
¼ tsp paprika
½ tsp sea salt
sunflower or vegetable oil, for frying
freshly ground black pepper

TIP: Don't over-process the falafel mixture – you're aiming for a grainy texture.

The addition of butternut squash makes these spicy falafel slightly sweet. Serve them piping hot with warm pitta or flatbreads, drizzled with tahini or yoghurt. They are great as part of a meze platter with hummus, tzatziki, juicy black olives, feta cubes and a Greek salad.

1 Put the dried chickpeas in a bowl and cover with plenty of cold water, as they will swell and double in size. Leave to soak overnight in a cool place. The following day, drain the chickpeas and pat them dry with kitchen paper (paper towels).

2 Put the squash in a microwave-safe bowl and cover with cling film (plastic wrap). Microwave on high for 10–12 minutes, or until tender. Allow to cool.

3 Blitz the chickpeas in a food processor for 1 minute. Add the butternut squash, along with the onion, chopped coriander and garlic. Pulse until well combined. Add the chickpea flour, baking powder, spices and salt and pulse until everything is chopped and binds together. If the mixture is too dry, add 2–3 tablespoons cold water; if it's too loose, add more flour. Season with black pepper and pulse again briefly.

4 Take tablespoons of the falafel mixture and, using your hands (dampen them with water if wished), shape them into balls. If you prefer, you can flatten the balls slightly to form patties. Place on a plate or plates, then cover and chill in the fridge for 30 minutes.

5 Pour enough oil into a deep, heavy-based saucepan to give a depth of 7.5cm/3in. Set over a medium to high heat and, when the temperature reaches 180°C/350°F (use a sugar thermometer to check), add the falafel, a few at a time so as not to overcrowd the pan. Fry for 4–5 minutes until crisp and golden brown, then remove with a slotted spoon and drain on a plate lined with kitchen paper while you cook the remaining falafel. Serve immediately.

PUMPKIN SEED TRAIL MIX

SERVES: 8 | **PREP:** 10 MINUTES

60g/2oz (scant ½ cup) almonds

60g/2oz (scant ½ cup) cashew nuts

60g/2oz (scant ½ cup) shelled pistachios

45g/1½oz (generous ¼ cup) pumpkin seeds

45g/1½oz (½ cup) coconut flakes

45g/1½oz (¼ cup) raisins

45g/1½oz (¼ cup) dried cranberries

100g/3½oz (1 cup) granola (preferably low-fat and reduced-sugar)

100g/3½oz (generous ½ cup) dark chocolate chips (70% cocoa solids)

Enjoy this delicious trail mix as a high-energy, high-protein snack, or sprinkle it over yoghurt and smoothie bowls.

1 Heat a dry frying pan (skillet) over a medium to high heat and add the nuts. They need to be in a single layer, so you may wish to do this in batches. Cook for 1–2 minutes, stirring or shaking the pan occasionally, until the nuts release their fragrance and are golden brown. Remove from the pan immediately before they catch and burn. Repeat with the pumpkin seeds.

2 Put the toasted nuts and seeds in a bowl and add all the other ingredients. Mix together well.

3 Transfer to a Mason or Kilner jar or a resealable bag and seal. This mixture keeps well for up to 3 weeks when stored in a cool, dry place.

OR YOU CAN TRY THIS...

– Add some dried goji berries, blueberries, cherries or chopped dates or apricots.

– Stir in some salty popcorn or a pinch of sea salt.

– Add cacao nibs instead of chocolate chips.

– Use peanuts instead of pistachios.

– Add some sesame or sunflower seeds.

TIP: Toasting the nuts and seeds gives them a distinctive flavour, but if you're in a hurry, just skip this step.

PUMPKIN SEED PESTO

SERVES: 4-6 | **PREP:** 10 MINUTES

30g/1oz (scant ¼ cup)
   pumpkin seeds
45g/1½oz (scant ½ cup)
   pine nuts
2 garlic cloves, crushed
a bunch of coriander
   (cilantro)
2 tbsp grated Parmesan
   cheese
juice of ½ lemon
120ml/4fl oz (½ cup) fruity
   green olive oil
salt and freshly ground
   black pepper
warm pitta bread triangles,
   to serve

Here's an unusual and delicious take on pesto using toasted pumpkin seeds. It's a great source of vegetable protein, vitamin K and B vitamins, as well as essential minerals, especially zinc.

1 Set a dry non-stick frying pan (skillet) over a medium heat. Add the pumpkin seeds and pine nuts and lightly toast, shaking the pan occasionally, for 1–2 minutes, or until they release their aroma and turn golden brown. Remove from the pan immediately, so they don't catch and burn.

2 Transfer the toasted pumpkin seeds and pine nuts to a blender or food processor, and add the garlic, coriander, Parmesan, lemon juice and most of the olive oil. Blitz to a paste, then drizzle the remaining olive oil through the feed tube, with the motor still running, until you get the desired consistency. Check the seasoning and add salt and pepper, if wished.

3 Transfer the pesto to a serving bowl or a sealed container and serve as a dip with warm pitta bread triangles. Alternatively, you can stir it into hot pasta.

OR YOU CAN TRY THIS...
– Add some unsalted cashew nuts.
– Use basil instead of coriander.
– Use the pesto as a spread for bread or crackers.
– Serve with raw vegetable dippers, e.g. chicory (Belgian endive), celery or carrots.

TRINIDAD SPICY PUMPKIN ROTI

SERVES: 4 | **PREP:** 30 MINUTES | **REST:** 1 HOUR | **COOK:** 45 MINUTES

225g/8oz (generous 2 cups)
self-raising (self-rising)
flour, sifted
a good pinch of ground
turmeric
½ tsp sea salt
1 tbsp sunflower oil, plus
extra for brushing and
frying
120ml/4fl oz (½ cup)
lukewarm water
West Indian hot sauce,
for drizzling

For the spicy pumpkin filling:
2 tbsp sunflower oil
1 onion, finely chopped
2 garlic cloves, crushed
400g/14oz pumpkin, peeled,
deseeded and diced
2 tsp curry powder
a pinch of ground allspice
120ml/4fl oz (½ cup)
coconut milk
1 x 400g/14oz can black
beans, rinsed and drained
100g/3½oz baby spinach
sea salt and freshly ground
black pepper

Roti is a popular snack and street food throughout the Caribbean – every island has its own version. You can also serve these as a light lunch or supper with fried plantains and rice.

1 To make the roti dough, put the flour, turmeric and salt in a mixing bowl and drizzle the oil over the top. Mix in the water, a little at a time, until you have a smooth, soft dough. If it's too dry, add some more water.

2 Knead the dough lightly for a few minutes, then cover and set aside to rest for at least 30 minutes.

3 Divide the dough into 8 equal-sized pieces and use a rolling pin to roll each one out into a thin circle. Lightly brush half of each circle with oil and fold it over. Brush half of the semi-circle with oil and fold again. Leave to rest for 30 minutes.

4 Meanwhile, make the filling. Heat the oil in a frying pan (skillet) set over a low to medium heat. Add the onion and garlic and cook for 6–8 minutes. Add the pumpkin and cook for a further 5 minutes, stirring occasionally. Stir in the curry powder and allspice and cook for 1 minute more. Add the coconut milk and black beans and simmer for 15 minutes, or until the vegetables are tender and the liquid has evaporated. Just before the end of the cooking time, stir in the spinach and season to taste.

5 Roll out the rotis into thin circles. Heat a little oil in a frying pan set over a medium to high heat. Fry the rotis, one at a time, for 2–3 minutes until golden brown underneath and puffy. Flip the roti over and cook on the other side. Set aside to drain on a plate lined with kitchen paper (paper towels) and keep warm while you fry the remaining rotis.

6 Divide the filling between the roti pancakes and fold over. Serve immediately, drizzled with hot sauce.

SICILIAN SQUASH CAPONATA

SERVES: 4 | **PREP:** 15 MINUTES | **COOK:** 1 HOUR

400g/14oz butternut squash,
   peeled, deseeded and
   cubed
3 tbsp olive oil, plus extra
   for drizzling
1 large onion, diced
3 garlic cloves, crushed
2 celery sticks, diced
1 red (bell) pepper, deseeded
   and cut into chunks
1 fennel bulb, diced
85ml/3fl oz (generous ¼ cup)
   red wine vinegar
60g/2oz (½ cup) sultanas
   (seedless golden raisins)
1 tbsp white sugar
1 x 400g (14oz) can
   chopped tomatoes
30g/1oz (scant ¼ cup) capers
60g/2oz (½ cup) stoned
   (pitted) black olives
45g/1½oz (scant ½ cup)
   pine nuts
a bunch of flat-leaf parsley,
   chopped
sea salt and freshly ground
   black pepper

TIP: You can store the caponata in a sealed container in the fridge for up to 3 days. It tastes even better on the second or third day.

This caponata is made with sweet butternut squash instead of aubergines (eggplants). It complements the *agrodolce* (sweet and sour) flavour of the sauce. Use it for topping bruschetta, or serve with grilled halloumi, chicken or fish.

1 Preheat the oven to 200°C/400°F/gas mark 6. Arrange the butternut squash on a baking tray (cookie sheet) and drizzle with olive oil. Roast for 20 minutes, or until tender.

2 Heat the oil in a large, deep frying pan (skillet) set over a medium heat. Add the onion, garlic, celery, red pepper and fennel and cook, stirring often, for 8–10 minutes until golden and tender. Stir in the roasted squash, along with the vinegar, sultanas and sugar and cook for a further 2–3 minutes. Add the tomatoes, capers and olives and season to taste.

3 Reduce the heat to low, then cover the pan with a lid and simmer gently, stirring occasionally, for 20–30 minutes, or until the vegetables are really tender and the liquid has reduced and thickened.

4 Meanwhile, toast the pine nuts in a small, dry frying pan set over a medium to high heat, tossing them gently, for 1–2 minutes, or until aromatic and golden brown. Remove from the pan before they catch and burn.

5 Stir the toasted pine nuts into the caponata, along with the parsley, and leave to cool. Serve lukewarm or at room temperature.

OR YOU CAN TRY THIS...
– Add a dash of harissa paste or diced chilli.
– Drizzle with good-quality balsamic vinegar before serving.
– Use pumpkin instead of butternut squash.

ROASTED SQUASH HUMMUS

SERVES: 4 | **PREP:** 15 MINUTES | **COOK:** 20 MINUTES

300g/10oz butternut
squash, peeled, deseeded
and cubed
3 tbsp olive oil, plus extra
for drizzling
1 x 400g/14oz can
chickpeas (garbanzos)
4 garlic cloves, crushed
2–3 tbsp tahini
grated zest and juice of
1 lemon, plus extra juice
for drizzling
a pinch of ground cumin
a pinch of hot paprika
sea salt and freshly ground
black pepper
toasted pumpkin seeds
or pomegranate seeds,
to serve

**This hummus has a lovely rich golden colour and is the perfect spread
or dip. It's delicious served with roasted baby carrots, red onion
wedges and fennel.**

1 Preheat the oven to 200°C/400°F/gas mark 6. Arrange the butternut
squash on a baking tray (cookie sheet) and drizzle with olive oil.
Roast in the oven for 20 minutes, or until tender. Set aside to cool.

2 Drain the chickpeas and reserve the liquid. Rinse the chickpeas in
a sieve under running cold water, then pat dry with kitchen paper
(paper towels).

3 Place the chickpeas, olive oil, garlic, tahini, lemon zest and juice and
cumin in a food processor or blender and blitz to combine. If you
wish, you can use a little of the reserved chickpea liquid to thin the
mixture to the consistency you want. It should be slightly grainy and
creamy. Season with salt and pepper.

4 Spoon the hummus into a shallow bowl and dust with paprika.
Drizzle with olive oil and lemon juice, then sprinkle with toasted
pumpkin seeds or pomegranate seeds. Serve with crusty bread,
crackers, pitta or flatbreads, or as a dip for tortilla chips or raw or
roasted vegetables.

TIP: This keeps well in
a sealed container in the
fridge for up to 4 days.

OR YOU CAN TRY THIS...
– Instead of butternut squash, use roasted pumpkin or red peppers.
– Serve sprinkled with dukkah or toasted pine nuts.
– Dust with cayenne pepper instead of paprika.
– For a creamier hummus, stir in some fat-free Greek yoghurt.
– If you're in a hurry, use canned pumpkin instead of roasting the
butternut squash.

PARMESAN PUMPKIN BITES

MAKES: 12 | **PREP:** 15 MINUTES | **COOK:** 20-25 MINUTES

butter or vegetable oil,
  for greasing
150g/5oz (1½ cups) self-
  raising (self-rising) flour
100g/3½oz (1 cup) grated
  Parmesan cheese
a pinch of grated nutmeg
450g/1lb (2 cups) mashed
  cooked pumpkin
  (see page 9)
2 medium free-range
  eggs, beaten
a handful of flat-leaf parsley,
  chopped
4 spring onions (scallions),
  diced
cayenne pepper or paprika,
  for dusting
sea salt and freshly ground
  black pepper

These light, cheesy bites make a tasty snack or savoury lunchbox treat. You could even eat them for breakfast, or serve as an appetiser with pre-dinner drinks. If you like, you could use mini muffin trays (pans) for smaller, bite-sized canapés.

1 Preheat the oven to 180°C/350°F/gas mark 4. Lightly butter or oil a 12-cup muffin tray (pan).

2 In a large bowl, mix together the flour, Parmesan and nutmeg. Make a well in the centre.

3 In another bowl, whisk together the mashed pumpkin and beaten eggs. Stir in the parsley and spring onions and season with salt and pepper. Pour this mixture into the well you created in the cheesy flour mixture. Fold in gently until everything is well combined.

4 Spoon the mixture into the prepared muffin tray and bake for 20 minutes, or until well risen and golden brown. Leave the muffins to cool in the pan for at least 5 minutes before easing them out and dusting lightly with cayenne pepper or paprika.

5 Eat them while they are still warm, or leave until cool and then store in an airtight container before reheating. They will keep well for up to 2 days in the fridge.

OR YOU CAN TRY THIS...
– Use mashed squash or sweet potato.
– Vary the herbs: try coriander (cilantro) or chives.
– Use a different hard cheese, e.g. Cheddar, Gruyère, Manchego or Pecorino.
– Add some pumpkin or fennel seeds.

BUTTERNUT SQUASH & FETA MUFFINS

MAKES: 12 | **PREP:** 20 MINUTES | **COOK:** 30-35 MINUTES

2 tbsp olive oil
1 small red onion, finely chopped
a pinch of ground cinnamon
100g/3½oz baby spinach, roughly torn
a few chives, snipped
250g/9oz (2½ cups) self-raising (self-rising) flour
1 tsp bicarbonate of soda (baking soda)
a good pinch of sea salt
2 medium free-range eggs, beaten
225g/8oz (1 cup) Greek yoghurt
100g/3½oz feta cheese, crumbled
225g/8oz butternut squash, grated
4 tbsp pumpkin seeds
2 tbsp pine nuts

TIP: To test whether the muffins are cooked, insert a thin skewer into the centre of a muffin – it should come out clean.

These green-flecked savoury muffins are perfect for a snack, an on-the-go breakfast or for brunch. The pumpkin seeds and nuts add crunch, while the spinach and squash keep the muffins lovely and moist.

1 Preheat the oven to 200°C/400°F/gas mark 6. Line a 12-cup muffin tray (pan) with paper cases (liners).

2 Heat the oil in a frying pan (skillet) set over a medium heat. Add the onion and cook for 6–8 minutes until softened. Stir in the cinnamon and spinach and cook for a further minute, then add the chives and set aside to cool.

3 Sift the flour, bicarbonate of soda and salt into a large mixing bowl. In a separate bowl, beat together the eggs and yoghurt, then stir this mixture into the flour, along with the onion and spinach mixture. Fold in the feta, butternut squash, pumpkin seeds and pine nuts.

4 Divide the mixture between the paper cases and bake for 20–25 minutes, or until well risen and golden brown.

5 Leave the muffins to cool in the tray for 5 minutes before transferring to a wire rack. Serve warm or at room temperature. They will keep well stored in an airtight container for up to 3 days. You can reheat them if you wish.

OR YOU CAN TRY THIS...
– Add some grated nutmeg, ground ginger or cumin.
– Sprinkle with seeds before baking.

DINNERS

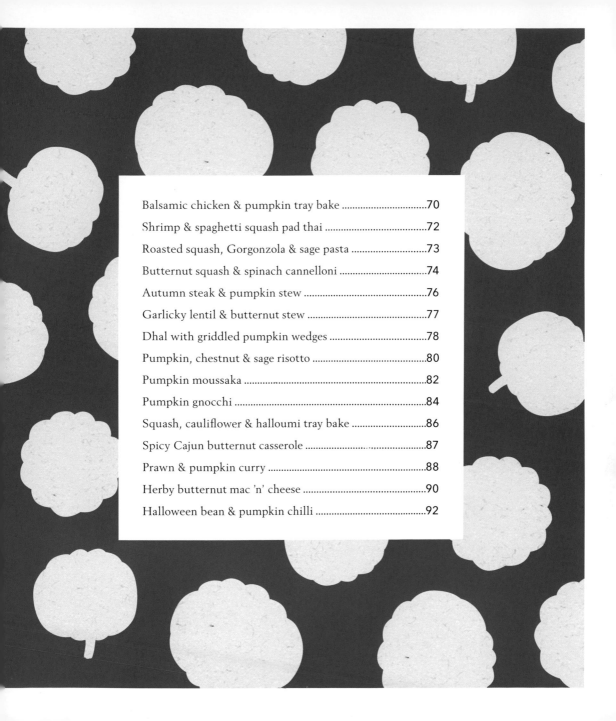

BALSAMIC CHICKEN & PUMPKIN TRAY BAKE

SERVES: 4 | **PREP:** 15 MINUTES | **COOK:** 40-50 MINUTES

3 tbsp olive oil
4 boneless chicken breasts
  (skin on)
2 red onions, cut into
  wedges
600g/1lb 5oz pumpkin,
  peeled, deseeded and cut
  into large chunks
300g/10oz cherry tomatoes
a few rosemary sprigs
4 garlic cloves, skin on
150ml/¼ pint (generous
  ½ cup) chicken stock
  (broth)
2 tbsp good-quality
  balsamic vinegar, plus
  extra for drizzling
a handful of parsley,
  chopped
sea salt and freshly ground
  black pepper

One-pan meals are so easy to prepare… and there's hardly any washing up. This is a great after-work supper when you're feeling tired. Use the best-quality balsamic vinegar you can find – a thick, syrupy one will give the best flavour.

1 Preheat the oven to 190°C/375°F/gas mark 5.

2 Heat the oil in a large roasting tray (pan) set over a medium heat on the hob. Add the chicken and cook for 8–10 minutes, turning occasionally, until browned all over.

3 Add the onions, pumpkin and tomatoes to the roasting tray. Tuck the rosemary and garlic into the gaps and pour the stock over the top. Sprinkle with the balsamic vinegar and season with salt and pepper.

4 Transfer the roasting tray to the oven and roast for 30–40 minutes, or until the chicken is cooked through, the vegetables are tender and the stock has almost evaporated.

5 Squeeze the garlic cloves out of their skins and stir into the vegetables. Sprinkle over the parsley and drizzle with some more balsamic vinegar, then serve.

OR YOU CAN TRY THIS...
– Use butternut squash or sweet potatoes instead of pumpkin.
– Drizzle with pomegranate molasses or hot sauce before serving.

BUTTERNUT SQUASH & SPINACH CANNELLONI

SERVES: 4 | **PREP:** 25 MINUTES | **COOK:** 1 HOUR

400g/14oz butternut squash, peeled, deseeded and cubed
olive oil, for drizzling
300g/10oz spinach, trimmed and roughly chopped
250g/9oz ricotta cheese
a good pinch of grated nutmeg
8 large or 16 small cannelloni tubes
200ml/7fl oz (generous ¾ cup) crème fraîche
60g/2oz (generous ½ cup) grated Parmesan cheese
sea salt and freshly ground black pepper

For the tomato sauce:
2 tbsp olive oil
1 large onion, finely chopped
2 garlic cloves, crushed
2 x 400g/14oz cans chopped tomatoes
2 tbsp tomato purée (paste)
1 tsp white sugar
a pinch of dried oregano
a splash of balsamic vinegar

You can prepare and assemble this delicious vegetarian pasta bake a few hours in advance. It's great with a crisp salad or green seasonal vegetables.

1 Preheat the oven to 200°C/400°F/gas mark 6. Line a baking tray (cookie sheet) with baking parchment.

2 Place the squash in a single layer on the lined baking tray. Drizzle with olive oil and season with salt and pepper. Roast for 25 minutes, or until tender. Remove from the oven and leave to cool. Reduce the oven temperature to 180°C/350°F/gas mark 4.

3 Meanwhile, make the tomato sauce. Heat the oil in a large frying pan (skillet) set over a low to medium heat. Add the onion and garlic and cook, stirring occasionally, for 6–8 minutes, or until softened. Add the tomatoes, tomato purée, sugar and oregano, then increase the heat to high. Let the sauce bubble away for 5–10 minutes, or until reduced and thickened. Add the balsamic vinegar and season to taste.

4 Put the spinach in a colander over the sink and pour a kettle of boiling water over it. When the spinach wilts and softens, press down on top of it with a saucer to extract all the water. Place on a board and chop coarsely.

5 Place the roasted squash in a large bowl and mash roughly with a potato masher. Stir in the ricotta, nutmeg and spinach. Season lightly with salt and pepper.

6 Fill the cannelloni tubes with the squash and spinach mixture, using a teaspoon or piping bag. Place the filled tubes in a large ovenproof dish and pour the tomato sauce over the top. Dot with spoonfuls of crème fraîche and sprinkle with Parmesan.

7 Bake for 35 minutes, or until the pasta is cooked and tender and the top is bubbling and golden brown. Serve hot with a salad.

DHAL WITH GRIDDLED PUMPKIN WEDGES

SERVES: 4 | **PREP:** 15 MINUTES | **COOK:** 40 MINUTES

2 tbsp sunflower oil
2 garlic cloves, crushed
2.5cm/1in piece of fresh root
  ginger, peeled and diced
1 red chilli, diced
1 tsp black mustard seeds
1 tsp ground turmeric
1 tsp garam masala
250g/9oz (1¼ cups) red
  lentils (dry weight)
480ml/16fl oz (2 cups) hot
  vegetable stock (broth)
400ml/14fl oz (scant 1¾
  cups) canned coconut milk
4 ripe tomatoes, roughly
  chopped
400g/14oz pumpkin,
  peeled, deseeded and cut
  into thin wedges
100g/3½oz baby spinach
juice of 1 lime
sea salt and freshly ground
  black pepper
naan bread or chapatis,
  to serve

For the tarka topping:
2 tbsp sunflower oil
1 large red onion, thinly
  sliced
1 tsp cumin seeds
1 red chilli, shredded
8 fresh curry leaves

When you feel in need of comfort food, make this spicy dhal. It's economical, healthy and delicious and never fails to warm you up. The griddled pumpkin adds a touch of contrasting colour and sweetness.

1 Heat 1 tablespoon of the oil in a large saucepan set over a low to medium heat. Add the garlic, ginger and chilli and cook for 2 minutes. Stir in the mustard seeds and ground spices; when the seeds start to pop, add the lentils, stock and coconut milk. Increase the heat to bring to the boil, then reduce the heat and simmer gently for 15 minutes.

2 Stir in the tomatoes and simmer for 15 minutes, or until the dhal is thick and creamy. If it's too liquid, simmer for another 5–10 minutes; if it's too thick, add more stock. Check the seasoning.

3 Meanwhile, make the tarka topping. Heat the oil in a frying pan (skillet) set over a low heat and cook the onion, stirring occasionally, for 12–15 minutes, or until it starts to caramelise and turn golden brown. Add the cumin seeds, chilli and curry leaves and cook for a further 2 minutes. Season with salt and pepper.

4 When the dhal is nearly ready, brush the pumpkin wedges with the remaining oil and cook in a large griddle pan set over a medium to high heat for 5 minutes on each side, or until tender and slightly charred.

5 Stir the spinach and lime juice into the dhal to wilt the spinach. Divide between 4 shallow bowls and top with the tarka mixture and griddled pumpkin wedges. Serve with warm naan or chapatis.

OR YOU CAN TRY THIS...
– Sprinkle with chopped coriander (cilantro) before serving.
– Serve with plain yoghurt or raita.
– Use butternut squash instead of pumpkin.

PUMPKIN, CHESTNUT & SAGE RISOTTO

SERVES: 4 | **PREP:** 15 MINUTES | **COOK:** 35-40 MINUTES

500g/1lb 2oz pumpkin,
    peeled, deseeded and cubed
olive oil, for drizzling
1.5 litres/2¾ pints (6½ cups)
    vegetable or chicken
    stock (broth)
60g/2oz (¼ cup) unsalted
    butter
1 onion, finely chopped
1 garlic clove, crushed
8 sage leaves, chopped
400g/14oz (scant 2 cups)
    risotto rice, e.g. Arborio
    or Carnaroli (dry weight)
60ml/2fl oz (¼ cup) white
    vermouth, e.g. Noilly Prat
100g/3½oz cooked chestnuts,
    shelled and chopped
sea salt and freshly ground
    black pepper
grated Parmesan cheese,
    to serve (optional)

For the mantecatura:
3 tbsp butter, diced
60g/2oz (generous ½ cup)
    grated Parmesan cheese

TIP: Use homemade stock, or the best-quality stock you can find. It will make all the difference to the flavour of the finished dish.

This risotto is eaten in northern Italy, especially in the Veneto region, in late autumn and winter when pumpkins are in season and the weather is cold. The pumpkin gives it sweetness, which is offset by the sage. Creamy, smooth and filling, this is the ultimate comfort food.

1 Preheat the oven to 200°C/400°F/gas mark 6. Line a baking tray (cookie sheet) with baking parchment.

2 Arrange the pumpkin cubes in a single layer on the lined baking tray and drizzle with olive oil. Season with salt and pepper, then roast for 30–35 minutes, or until tender.

3 Meanwhile, heat the stock in a saucepan over a medium to high heat. When it starts to boil, turn the heat down as low as it will go.

4 Melt the butter in a large, deep frying pan (skillet) set over a low heat. Add the onion and garlic and cook, stirring occasionally, for 10 minutes, or until softened. Add the sage and cook for 1 minute more, then stir in the rice. When all the grains of rice are glistening and starting to crackle, increase the heat to medium and add the vermouth – it will hiss and steam. Cook for 4–5 minutes until the liquid evaporates and is absorbed by the rice.

5 Reduce the heat to low and start adding the warm stock, a ladleful at a time. Stir well and wait for it to be absorbed before adding another ladleful. Continue until the rice is tender but still retains a little bite (al dente) and all or most of the stock has been added. Remove from the heat.

6 Mash the roasted pumpkin coarsely with a potato masher or fork and stir into the risotto.

7 Now add the *mantecatura*. Vigorously beat in the butter and Parmesan until the risotto is creamy. Finally, stir in the chestnuts and leave to 'rest' for 2–3 minutes before serving in shallow bowls, sprinkled with Parmesan (if using).

PUMPKIN MOUSSAKA

SERVES: 4-6 | **PREP:** 20 MINUTES | **COOK:** 1¼-1½ HOURS

600g/1lb 5oz pumpkin,
  peeled and deseeded
plain flour, for dusting
6 tbsp olive oil, plus extra
  for brushing
1 red onion, chopped
2 garlic cloves, crushed
500g/1lb 2oz (2¼ cups)
  minced (ground) beef
½ tsp grated nutmeg
½ tsp ground cinnamon
2 tbsp tomato purée (paste)
1 x 400g/14oz can chopped
  tomatoes
1 tsp white sugar
a pinch of dried oregano
120ml/4fl oz (½ cup)
  red wine
60g/2oz (generous ½ cup)
  grated Graviera or
  Parmesan cheese
sea salt and freshly ground
  black pepper

Using pumpkin in place of the traditional aubergine (eggplant) in a moussaka makes it sweeter and less oily. Serve it lukewarm, with a crisp green salad or a Greek country salad (*horiatiki*).

1 Preheat the oven to 180°C/350°F/gas mark 4.

2 Cut the pumpkin into 6mm/¼in slices. Dust the slices lightly with flour, shaking off any excess. Heat 4 tablespoons of the oil in a large frying pan (skillet) set over a medium heat and fry the pumpkin, a few slices a time, for 2 minutes on each side, or until golden brown. Set aside on a plate lined with kitchen paper (paper towels) to drain.

3 Heat the remaining oil in a saucepan set over a medium heat. Add the onion and garlic and cook, stirring occasionally, for 6–8 minutes until softened. Add the beef and cook for a further 5 minutes until browned all over. Stir in the ground spices and cook for 1 minute more, then add the tomato purée, tomatoes, sugar, oregano and red wine. Bring to the boil, then reduce the heat to low and simmer gently for 15 minutes, or until the liquid has evaporated and the sauce has thickened. Season to taste with salt and pepper.

4 Meanwhile, make the white sauce. Melt the butter in a saucepan set over a low heat and stir in the flour to create a paste. Cook for 1 minute, then start whisking in the milk, a little at a time, until everything has been added and there are no lumps. Increase the heat to high and bring to the boil, still whisking, then reduce the heat to low and cook for a further 5–10 minutes until the sauce is thick, glossy and smooth. Remove from the heat and beat in the egg yolks quickly. Season to taste.

For the white sauce:
100g/3½oz (scant ½ cup)
    butter
100g/3½oz (1 cup) plain
    (all-purpose) flour
750ml/1¼ pints (generous
    3 cups) milk
2 egg yolks, beaten

5 Lightly brush a large ovenproof dish with oil and cover the base with half of the pumpkin slices. Spoon the beef mixture over the top, then cover with the remaining pumpkin slices. Pour over the white sauce and sprinkle with the grated cheese.

6 Bake for 40–45 minutes, or until the top of the moussaka is golden brown. Remove from the oven and leave to cool for at least 10 minutes before cutting into portions and serving. It is best eaten lukewarm with a salad on the side.

OR YOU CAN TRY THIS...
– Use butternut squash or sweet potato instead of pumpkin.
– Add some grated cheese to the white sauce.

TIP: It's important to let the moussaka cool down before cutting – the sauce sets as it cools and becomes firm.

PUMPKIN GNOCCHI

SERVES: 4 | **PREP:** 25 MINUTES | **CHILL:** 15 MINUTES | **COOK:** 1–1¼ HOURS

600g/1lb 5oz pumpkin
400g/14oz sweet potatoes,
    scrubbed and pierced
    with a skewer
olive oil, for drizzling
200g/7oz (2 cups) plain
    (all-purpose) flour, plus
    extra for dusting
2 tsp baking powder
¼ tsp sea salt
a good pinch of grated
    nutmeg
1 large free-range egg, beaten
60g/2oz (generous ½ cup)
    grated Parmesan cheese

To serve:
60g/2oz (¼ cup) unsalted
    butter
12 sage leaves
shaved Parmesan cheese,
    for sprinkling
freshly grated black pepper

TIP: If the ball of dough is too moist, add some more flour to bind it together. If it's too dry, add some more beaten egg.

Gnocchi are usually made from potatoes or semolina, but these gloriously coloured pumpkin gnocchi are a staple dish in Venice and the Veneto region during the winter.

1 Preheat the oven to 200°C/400°F/gas mark 6. Line a baking tray (cookie sheet) with baking parchment

2 Cut the pumpkin into large wedges and discard the seeds. Lie the wedges on their sides on the lined baking tray, along with the sweet potatoes. Drizzle with olive oil and bake for 50–60 minutes, or until tender.

3 When they are cool enough to handle, remove the outer peel from the pumpkin wedges and scoop out the sweet potato flesh from the skins. Place the pumpkin and sweet potato flesh in a large bowl and mash with a potato masher, or purée using a food mill or potato ricer.

4 Put the flour, baking powder, salt and nutmeg in a mixing bowl and stir in the pumpkin and sweet potato purée with a wooden spoon. Mix in the beaten egg and cheese. When the mixture comes together to form a sticky ball, turn it out onto a lightly floured surface and knead until smooth. Cover and chill in the fridge for at least 15 minutes.

5 Divide the dough into 4 pieces and, on a floured board, roll each one out to form a long cylinder. Cut each cylinder into 2cm/¾in lengths and then, if you wish, slide them lightly over the tines of a fork to create a ridged surface on one side.

6 Drop the gnocchi, a few at a time, into a large saucepan of boiling salted water. As soon as they rise to the surface, after 1–2 minutes, remove with a slotted spoon and drain well. Transfer to a separate dish and keep warm.

7 Melt the butter in a large frying pan (skillet) over a low to medium heat and add the sage. When the leaves start to crisp and release their aroma, pour the melted sage butter over the gnocchi. Serve immediately, sprinkled with shaved Parmesan and a grinding of black pepper.

SQUASH, CAULIFLOWER & HALLOUMI TRAY BAKE

SERVES: 4 | **PREP:** 20 MINUTES | **COOK:** 35-45 MINUTES

1 large cauliflower, stalk
    trimmed and leaves
    removed
1 tsp ground coriander
1 tsp ground cumin
½ tsp ground turmeric
4 tbsp olive oil
450g/1lb butternut squash,
    peeled, deseeded and
    cubed
150g/5oz cherry tomatoes
250g/9oz halloumi, sliced
green pesto, for drizzling
sea salt and freshly ground
    black pepper
couscous, quinoa or rice,
    to serve

Another simple supper cooked in a roasting tray (pan). All you have to do is prepare the vegetables and assemble it, then put your feet up while it cooks. A quick flash under a hot grill (broiler) at the end, and it's ready to eat.

1 Preheat the oven to 200°C/400°F/gas mark 6.

2 Slice the cauliflower through the stem into 4 thick 'steaks'. In a small bowl, mix the spices with 2 tablespoons of the olive oil. Brush this mixture over both sides of the cauliflower steaks.

3 Arrange the cauliflower steaks in a large roasting tray (pan). Place the squash and tomatoes around them and drizzle with the remaining olive oil. Season lightly with salt and pepper.

4 Bake for 30–40 minutes, or until the squash is tender and the cauliflower is golden brown around the edges.

5 Add the halloumi to the tray and place under a hot grill (broiler) for at least 5 minutes until the cheese is hot and golden brown.

6 Serve immediately, drizzled with pesto, with some couscous, quinoa or rice on the side.

OR YOU CAN TRY THIS...

– Use pumpkin or sweet potato instead of squash.
– Drizzle with pomegranate molasses or balsamic vinegar before serving.

SPICY CAJUN BUTTERNUT CASSEROLE

SERVES: 4 | **PREP:** 20 MINUTES | **COOK:** 1 HOUR

3 tbsp olive oil

2 red onions, cut into thin wedges

4 garlic cloves, crushed

2 red or yellow (bell) peppers, deseeded and cut into chunks

900g/2lb butternut squash, peeled, deseeded and cubed

1 tbsp Cajun seasoning

½ tsp ground cumin

180ml/6fl oz (¾ cup) vegetable stock (broth)

400ml/14fl oz (scant 1¾ cups) canned coconut milk

1 x 400g/14oz can chopped tomatoes

1 tsp dark molasses sugar

1 x 400g/14oz can black beans, rinsed and drained

300g/10oz spinach, trimmed and shredded

sea salt and freshly ground black pepper

cooked brown rice or warm griddled flatbreads, to serve

This gently spiced Caribbean dish is a hybrid – a cross between a soup and a stew. It makes a delicious supper, or you can make double the quantity to serve to your guests at a Halloween or Bonfire Night party.

1 Heat the oil in a large saucepan or flameproof casserole set over a low to medium heat. Add the red onions, garlic and peppers and cook, stirring occasionally, for 8–10 minutes, or until softened. Stir in the butternut squash, Cajun seasoning and cumin and cook for a further 5 minutes.

2 Add the stock and coconut milk and bring to the boil. Reduce the heat to low and stir in the tomatoes, sugar and black beans. Simmer gently for 30–40 minutes, or until the liquid reduces and thickens, and the squash is cooked and tender but keeps its shape.

3 Stir in the spinach and cook for 5 minutes until it wilts and softens. Season to taste with salt and pepper.

4 Serve ladled into shallow bowls, with brown rice or griddled flatbreads on the side.

OR YOU CAN TRY THIS...

– For a creamy texture, stir in 4–5 tablespoons crème fraîche at the end.
– Sprinkle with chopped coriander (cilantro) before serving.
– Use pumpkin or sweet potato instead of squash.

TIP: You can buy Cajun seasoning in most supermarkets and delis.

PRAWN & PUMPKIN CURRY

SERVES: 4 | **PREP:** 20 MINUTES | **COOK:** 25-30 MINUTES

2 tbsp groundnut (peanut)
   oil
1 large onion, chopped
3 garlic cloves, crushed
2.5cm/1in piece of fresh
   root ginger, peeled
   and grated
2 tbsp Thai red curry paste
400ml/14fl oz (scant 1¾
   cups) canned coconut milk
300ml/½ pint (1¼ cups)
   hot fish or chicken stock
   (broth)
1 tsp coconut sugar
1 tbsp nam pla (Thai fish
   sauce)
400g/14oz pumpkin,
   peeled, deseeded and
   cubed
500g/1lb 2oz peeled large
   raw prawns (jumbo
   shrimp)
300g/10oz shredded
   spinach
juice of 1 lime
a handful of coriander
   (cilantro), chopped
boiled or steamed rice,
   to serve
shredded red chilli and
   lime wedges, to serve

This fragrant and colourful Thai curry is easy to make for a weekday supper. Keep some prawns (shrimp) in the freezer ready to defrost, or you could use a bag of frozen seafood (prawns, squid and scallops or mussels).

1 Heat the oil in a large saucepan or wok set over a medium to high heat. Add the onion, garlic and ginger and stir-fry for 4–5 minutes, or until the onion is tender. Stir in the curry paste and cook for 1 minute more.

2 Add the coconut milk, hot stock, sugar and nam pla, then reduce the heat and stir in the pumpkin. Cook gently for 15 minutes, or until the pumpkin is cooked through but not mushy and the sauce has reduced.

3 Add the prawns and cook for 3–4 minutes, turning them in the sauce, until they turn pink. Stir in the spinach and cook for a further 1–2 minutes, or until it wilts. Finally, stir in the lime juice and most of the coriander.

4 Serve immediately on a mound of rice, sprinkled with the remaining coriander and some shredded chilli, with lime wedges on the side for squeezing.

OR YOU CAN TRY THIS...
– Serve with rice noodles instead of rice.
– Use green curry paste instead of red.
– Substitute butternut squash for the pumpkin.

TIP: Coconut milk is quite high in fat, so why not use a reduced-fat brand?

HERBY BUTTERNUT MAC 'N' CHEESE

SERVES: 4 | **PREP:** 20 MINUTES | **COOK:** 50 MINUTES

600g/1lb 5oz butternut
squash, peeled, deseeded
and cubed
olive oil, for drizzling
leaves from 3 thyme sprigs
300g/10oz macaroni
(dry weight)
3 tbsp unsalted butter
1 large onion, finely
chopped
2 garlic cloves, crushed
60g/2oz (generous ½ cup)
plain (all-purpose) flour
500ml/17fl oz (2 cups) milk
1 tsp Dijon mustard
½ tsp grated nutmeg
a handful of flat-leaf parsley,
finely chopped
60g/2oz (generous ½ cup)
grated Cheddar cheese
60g/2oz (1 cup) fresh
breadcrumbs
a pinch of crushed dried
chilli flakes
sea salt and freshly ground
black pepper

This variation on a classic macaroni cheese makes a delicious and economical family supper. Serve it with a crisp salad or some steamed green vegetables.

1 Preheat the oven to 200°C/400°F/gas mark 6. Line a baking tray (cookie sheet) with baking parchment.

2 Arrange the squash in a single layer on the lined baking tray. Drizzle with oil and sprinkle with the thyme, then season with salt and pepper. Roast for 25 minutes, turning halfway through, or until tender.

3 Meanwhile, cook the macaroni according to the instructions on the packet. Drain well.

4 Melt the butter in a saucepan set over a low to medium heat. Add the onion and garlic and cook, stirring occasionally, for 8–10 minutes, or until tender. Reduce the heat to low and stir in the flour. Cook for 1 minute, then start adding the milk, a little at a time, stirring and whisking until smooth and free from floury lumps. Cook gently for 4–5 minutes until the white sauce thickens. Stir in the mustard, nutmeg, parsley and most of the grated cheese. Season to taste with salt and pepper.

5 Stir the cooked macaroni and roasted squash into the sauce and transfer to a large ovenproof dish. Sprinkle the breadcrumbs, chilli flakes and remaining cheese over the top, then drizzle with oil.

6 Bake for 20–25 minutes, or until bubbling and crisp and golden brown on top. Serve immediately.

OR YOU CAN TRY THIS...
– Use Gruyère or Parmesan instead of Cheddar.
– Use pumpkin instead of squash.

HALLOWEEN BEAN & PUMPKIN CHILLI

SERVES: 4 | **PREP:** 15 MINUTES | **COOK:** 45-55 MINUTES

3 tbsp olive oil
1 large red onion, chopped
3 garlic cloves, crushed
2 red (bell) peppers,
    deseeded and diced
675g/1lb 8oz pumpkin,
    peeled, deseeded and cubed
2–3 tsp chilli powder or
    2 tbsp chipotle paste
1 tsp ground cumin
1 tsp ground coriander
½ tsp ground cinnamon
½ tsp dried oregano
2 tbsp tomato purée (paste)
1 x 400g/14oz can chopped
    tomatoes
2 x 400g/14oz cans black
    beans, rinsed and drained
600ml/1 pint (2½ cups)
    vegetable stock (broth)
a handful of coriander
    (cilantro), chopped
sea salt and freshly ground
    black pepper
boiled or steamed rice,
    to serve (optional)
lime wedges, to serve

For the toppings:
chopped avocado
diced spring onions (scallions)
sour cream
grated Cheddar cheese
guacamole or tomato salsa

This is the perfect warming supper for a Halloween party after trick-or-treating outside on a cold evening. You can make the chilli in advance and reheat it when you get back home, or make it in a slow cooker (see tip below).

1 Heat the oil in a large saucepan set over a low to medium heat. Add the onion, garlic, peppers and pumpkin and cook, stirring occasionally, for 10–12 minutes, or until tender.

2 Stir in the chilli powder or chipotle paste, along with the ground cumin, coriander and cinnamon. Cook for 1 minute, then add the oregano, tomato purée, tomatoes, black beans and vegetable stock. Increase the heat to bring to a boil, then reduce the heat to low and simmer gently for 30–40 minutes, or until the liquid reduces and thickens.

3 Season to taste with salt and pepper, and stir in the chopped coriander.

4 Serve the chilli in shallow bowls with rice (if liked), and lime wedges on the side for squeezing. Everyone can help themselves to the toppings.

OR YOU CAN TRY THIS...
– Use red kidney beans instead of black beans.
– Substitute butternut squash or sweet potato for the pumpkin.
– Serve with griddled tortillas or tortilla chips.

TIP: If you're making this in a slow cooker, cook the onion, garlic and peppers in the oil until softened, then transfer to a slow cooker and add the remaining ingredients. Cover and cook on low for 5 hours.

BAKING & DESSERTS

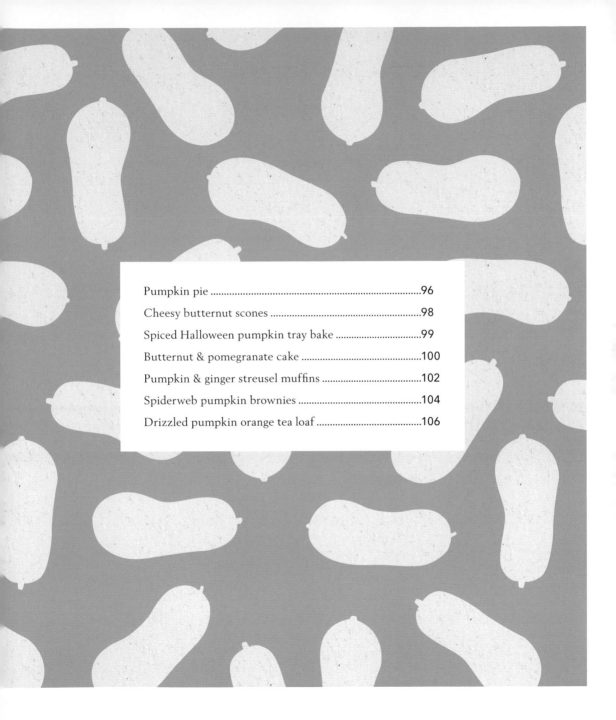

PUMPKIN PIE

SERVES: 8 | **PREP:** 40 MINUTES | **CHILL:** 30 MINUTES | **COOK:** 1½–1¾ HOURS

butter, for greasing
1 small dessert pumpkin,
    approx. 500g/1lb 2oz
150g/5oz (¾ cup) soft
    brown sugar
2 large free-range eggs,
    plus 1 egg yolk
1 tsp ground cinnamon,
    plus extra for dusting
½ tsp ground ginger
¼ tsp ground cloves
¼ tsp grated nutmeg
grated zest of 1 lemon
240ml/8fl oz (1 cup)
    evaporated milk
whipped cream, to serve

*For the shortcrust pastry
(pie crust):*
200g/7oz (2 cups) plain
    (all-purpose) flour
a pinch of sea salt
100g/3½oz (scant ½ cup)
    chilled butter, diced

TIP: If you are pressed for
time, you can cheat and
use canned pumpkin (one
450g/1lb can) and a shop-
bought pie shell.

**No Thanksgiving celebration feast would be complete without a
traditional pumpkin pie, and many people now bake it for Halloween, too.**

1 Preheat the oven to 200°C/400°F/gas mark 6. Lightly butter a
  23cm/9in tart tin (pan). Line a baking tray (cookie sheet) with
  baking parchment or foil.

2 Cut the pumpkin in half horizontally and remove the seeds. Place the
  pumpkin halves, cut-side down, on the lined baking tray and bake for
  30–40 minutes, or until tender. Remove and leave to cool.

3 Meanwhile, make the pastry. Sift the flour and salt into a mixing
  bowl. Rub in the butter until the mixture resembles breadcrumbs.
  Stir in 3–4 tablespoons cold water with a palette knife until the
  mixture forms a dough. Mould it into a ball, wrap it in cling film
  (plastic wrap) and chill in the fridge for at least 30 minutes.

4 Roll out the pastry on a lightly floured surface and use it to line the
  tart tin, pressing it into the sides. Level the top. Place a sheet of baking
  parchment inside and fill with baking beans. Bake 'blind' for 15
  minutes, then remove the parchment and beans. Return the crust to
  the oven for 5 minutes, or until the base is golden brown. Remove from
  the oven and reduce the temperature to 180°C/350°F/gas mark 4.

5 Scoop the roasted pumpkin out of the skin – you want around
  300g/10oz pumpkin. Place in a food processor and blitz until smooth.

6 In a large bowl, beat the sugar, eggs and egg yolk. Stir in the spices and
  lemon zest. Add the pumpkin purée and stir in the evaporated milk.

7 Pour into the pastry case and bake for 45 minutes, or until the filling
  sets. Don't worry if it's still a little wobbly – it will firm up as it cools.
  Leave to cool in the tin on a wire rack for 1–2 hours.

8 Cut the pie into slices and serve with whipped cream and a dusting
  of cinnamon. It will keep well in the fridge for 24 hours.

BUTTERNUT & POMEGRANATE CAKE

SERVES: 8-10 | **PREP:** 25 MINUTES | **COOK:** 1¼ HOURS

400g/14oz butternut
  squash, peeled, deseeded
  and cubed
3 free-range medium eggs
200g/7oz (1 cup) soft
  brown sugar
120ml/4fl oz (½ cup)
  sunflower oil, plus extra
  for greasing
300g/10oz (3 cups) plain
  (all-purpose) flour
1 heaped tsp baking powder
½ tsp bicarbonate of soda
  (baking soda)
1 tsp ground cinnamon
½ tsp ground cardamom
a pinch of sea salt
75g/3oz (¾ cup) chopped
  pistachios
seeds of 1 small pomegranate

For the white chocolate icing:
60ml/2fl oz (¼ cup) double
  (heavy) cream
115g/4oz white chocolate,
  broken into squares

This moist and gently spiced cake is made with oil instead of butter and is attractively flecked with colourful pistachios and pomegranate seeds. The creamy white chocolate icing adds the perfect finishing touch.

1 Preheat the oven to 180°C/350°F/gas mark 4. Lightly oil a 450g/1lb loaf tin (pan) and line with baking parchment.

2 Cook the squash in a saucepan of boiling water for 15–20 minutes, or until tender. Drain well and mash with a potato masher, or blend with a stick blender.

3 Place the eggs, sugar and oil in a food processor and beat until well blended. Sift in the flour, baking powder, bicarbonate of soda, spices and salt. Mix together gently on a low speed, then add the mashed butternut squash. Stir in the pistachios and pomegranate seeds with a spoon, reserving a few to decorate the finished cake.

4 Pour the mixture into the prepared tin and level the top. Bake for 1 hour, or until the cake rises and is golden brown. Test whether it is cooked by inserting a thin skewer into the centre – it should come out clean. Cool in the tin for 15 minutes, then turn out onto a wire rack to cool completely.

5 To make the icing, heat the cream in a small saucepan over a medium heat. When it starts to boil, remove from the heat and stir in the chocolate. When the chocolate melts and the mixture is smooth, pour or drizzle it over the cake, then scatter over the reserved pistachios and pomegranate seeds. Leave the icing to set, then cut the cake into slices to serve. Store in an airtight container in the fridge for up to 5 days.

OR YOU CAN TRY THIS...
– Add 2 tablespoons cocoa powder or a few drops of vanilla extract to the cake mixture.
– Use chopped hazelnuts, walnuts or pecans.

PUMPKIN & GINGER STREUSEL MUFFINS

MAKES: 12 | **PREP:** 20 MINUTES | **COOK:** 20 MINUTES

200g/7oz (2 cups) plain (all-purpose) flour
1 tsp baking powder
1 tsp bicarbonate of soda (baking soda)
1 tsp ground cinnamon
1 tsp grated nutmeg
½ tsp ground allspice
½ tsp sea salt
175g/6oz (¾ cup) butter, at room temperature
200g/7oz (1 cup) brown sugar
2 medium free-range eggs
400g/14oz (1¾ cups) pumpkin purée
2 tbsp milk
2 knobs preserved stem ginger in syrup, diced

For convenience, you can use canned pumpkin purée to make these crunchy topped, spicy muffins, or you can cut up some leftover pumpkin and boil it until tender before puréeing (see page 9).

1 Preheat the oven to 190°C/375°F/gas mark 5. Fill a 12-hole muffin tin (pan) with paper cases (liners).

2 Sift the flour, baking powder, bicarbonate of soda, ground spices and salt into a bowl and mix together well.

3 In a separate large mixing bowl, beat together the butter and sugar with a hand-held electric whisk until light and fluffy. Beat in the eggs, one at a time, followed by the pumpkin purée and milk. Stir in the stem ginger. Gently fold in the flour and spice mixture until everything is well combined. Do not beat or overmix. Spoon the mixture into the paper cases.

4 To make the streusel topping, mix together the flour, cinnamon, salt, sugar and walnuts in a bowl. Stir in the melted butter and ginger syrup. Sprinkle this mixture over the top of the muffins, pressing it slightly into the mixture.

For the streusel topping:
45g/1½oz (scant ½ cup)
   plain flour
½ tsp ground cinnamon
a pinch of sea salt
60g/2oz (¼ cup) demerara
   sugar
100g/3½oz (¾ cup)
   chopped walnuts
85g/3oz (⅓ cup) butter,
   melted
1½ tsp ginger syrup (from
   the stem ginger jar)
icing (confectioner's) sugar,
   for dusting

5 Bake for 20 minutes, or until the muffins are cooked through, golden brown and crunchy on top. You can test whether they are ready by inserting a thin skewer into the centre of a muffin – it should come out clean.

6 Leave to cool in the tin for 10 minutes, then transfer to a wire rack to cool completely. Once the muffins are cool, dust with icing sugar. Store in an airtight container in the fridge for up to 5 days.

OR YOU CAN TRY THIS...
– Use butternut squash instead of pumpkin.
– Use pumpkin pie spice instead of a mix of ground spices.
– Vary the nuts: try pecans, hazelnuts or almonds.

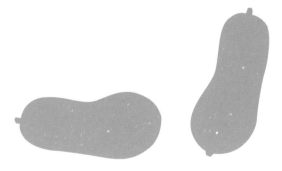

SPIDERWEB PUMPKIN BROWNIES

MAKES: 9 | **PREP:** 20 MINUTES | **COOK:** 20-25 MINUTES

250g/9oz (generous 1 cup) unsalted butter, cubed, plus extra for greasing
250g/9oz dark chocolate (70% cocoa solids), broken into squares
250g/9oz (1¼ cups) light brown sugar
3 medium free-range eggs
150g/5oz (1½ cups) self-raising (self-rising) flour, sifted
250g/9oz (1 generous cup) pumpkin purée

For the spiderweb icing:
250g/9oz (2 cups) icing (confectioner's) sugar
85g/3oz dark chocolate, broken into squares

These brownies are the perfect treat for trick-or-treaters on Halloween. Use canned puréed pumpkin or make your own (see page 9).

1 Preheat the oven to 170°C/325°F, gas mark 3. Lightly butter a 23 x 23cm/9 x 9in baking tin (pan) and line with baking parchment.

2 Place the butter and chocolate in a heatproof bowl. Suspend the bowl over a saucepan of simmering water. When the butter and chocolate melt, stir gently until well combined.

3 In a bowl, beat together the sugar and eggs until creamy with a hand-held electric whisk. Add the melted chocolate and butter and stir until amalgamated, then fold in the flour. Add the pumpkin purée and stir gently until smooth. Do not overmix.

4 Spoon the mixture into the lined tin and smooth the top. Bake for 20–25 minutes until cooked through and firm on top. Leave to cool in the tin, standing on a wire rack.

5 To make the icing, sift the icing sugar into a bowl and gradually stir in 2 tablespoons warm water, a little at a time, until smooth and thick enough to coat the back of the spoon. Spoon into a piping bag fitted with a thin plain nozzle.

6 Melt the chocolate in a heatproof bowl suspended over a saucepan of gently simmering water.

7 Cut the cooled brownies into 9 squares and remove from the tin. Cover the top of each brownie with the melted chocolate. Pipe a little circle of icing in the centre of each brownie and then pipe 3 concentric circles round it. Drag a toothpick or thin skewer from the centre through the circles to the edge at equal intervals to create a spiderweb effect.

8 Leave for 10 minutes or so until the icing sets. The brownies will keep well in an airtight container in the fridge for 4–5 days.

DRIZZLED PUMPKIN ORANGE TEA LOAF

MAKES: 900G/2LB LOAF | **PREP:** 20 MINUTES | **COOK:** 50-60 MINUTES

butter, for greasing
200g/7oz (1 cup) light
    brown sugar
4 medium free-range eggs,
    separated
250g/9oz pumpkin, peeled,
    deseeded and grated
grated zest and juice of
    1 small orange
a few drops of vanilla extract
75g/3oz (generous ½ cup)
    chopped walnuts
75g/3oz (½ cup) ready-to-eat
    dried apricots, chopped
200g/7oz (2 cups) self-raising
    (self-rising) flour
a pinch of sea salt
1 tsp ground cinnamon
½ tsp ground ginger
100g/3½oz (⅔ cup) ground
    almonds

For the orange drizzle:
125g/4oz (1 cup) icing
    (confectioner's) sugar
2 tbsp orange juice
grated zest of ½ orange

This tea loaf is moist, healthy and delicious. If you wish, you can forget the frosting and just dust it with icing sugar. You can enjoy it sliced and plain, or spread with butter at breakfast or teatime, or as a snack.

1 Preheat the oven to 170°C/325°F/gas mark 3. Lightly grease and line a 900g/2lb loaf tin (pan) with baking parchment.

2 In a bowl, beat together the sugar and egg yolks until fluffy, pale and creamy. Add the grated pumpkin, along with the orange zest and juice, vanilla, walnuts and apricots. Sift the flour, salt and spices and fold into the mixture, along with the ground almonds, moving the spoon in a figure-of-eight movement.

3 In a clean, dry bowl, beat the egg whites until they form soft peaks, then fold gently into the pumpkin mixture. Do not beat or overmix.

4 Spoon the mixture into the lined tin and bake for 50–60 minutes, or until well risen and golden brown. You can check whether the cake is cooked by inserting a thin skewer into the middle – it should come out clean. Leave to cool in the tin for 5 minutes, then turn out and cool completely on a wire rack.

5 To make the orange drizzle, mix the icing sugar and orange juice together in a bowl until smooth. Drizzle over the top of the loaf and then scatter over the orange zest. Leave to set.

6 Cut into slices to serve. The loaf will keep well in an airtight container in the fridge for up to 5 days, or in a cool place for 2–3 days.

OR YOU CAN TRY THIS...

– Use raisins, dates or dried cranberries instead of apricots.
– Use chopped pecans, hazelnuts or almonds.
– Use butternut squash instead of pumpkin.

INDEX

1

Published in 2021 by Ebury Press an imprint of Ebury Publishing,
20 Vauxhall Bridge Road,
London SW1V 2SA

Ebury Press is part of the Penguin Random House group of companies
whose addresses can be found at global.penguinrandomhouse.com

Text copyright © Ebury Press 2021
Photography copyright © Ebury Press 2021
Design copyright © Ebury Press 2021

Design: Louise Evans
Photography: Joff Lee
Food Styling: Mari Williams
Prop Styling: Rachel Vere
Editor: Camilla Ackley

This edition first published by Ebury Press in 2021

www.penguin.co.uk

A CIP catalogue record for this book is available from the British Library

ISBN 9781529148046

Printed and bound in China by Toppan Leefung

The authorised representative in the EEA is Penguin Random House Ireland,
Morrison Chambers, 32 Nassau Street, Dublin D02 YH68

Penguin Random House is committed to a sustainable future for our business,
our readers and our planet. This book is made from Forest Stewardship Council®
certified paper.